MICHIGAN ROSS SCHOOL OF BUSINESS

A Century of Stories Celebrating the "Leaders and Best"

GEORGE SIEDEL
University of Michigan

Van Rye
PUBLISHING

Copyright © 2025 George Siedel

All rights reserved. No part of this book may be reproduced, stored in a retrieval system, or transmitted—in any form or by any means (electronic, mechanical, photocopying, recording, or otherwise)—without prior written permission from the publisher, except in the case of brief quotations in articles or reviews.

Cover design by Vila Design

Published by Van Rye Publishing, LLC
Ann Arbor, MI
www.vanryepublishing.com

ISBN: 978-1-957906-18-8 (paperback)
ISBN: 978-1-957906-19-5 (ebook)
Library of Congress Control Number: 2024950350

Praise for *Michigan Ross School of Business*

"Fascinating history, engaging stories, excellent writing by a great professor!"
—B. Joseph White, President Emeritus, University of Illinois and Dean Emeritus, University of Michigan

"A necessary read not just for those interested in the history of Michigan Ross but also for those seeking to develop an understanding of how great institutions are built."
—Gautam Ahuja, Eleanora and George Landew Professor of Management, Cornell University

"I hope that others will find inspiration here to aim high in their work and, so doing, fill the pages of another book like this in 50 or 100 years."
—Jim Walsh, Gerald and Esther Carey Professor of Business Administration, University of Michigan, and Past President, Academy of Management

"With meticulous research and gifted storytelling, Siedel evokes the majesty of Michigan Ross and distills the ingredients of its success."
—Leigh Anenson, Professor, University of Maryland and Past-President, Academy of Legal Studies in Business

"An amazing contribution both to Ross and to the University; I stayed up most of the night reading the book and could not put it down."
—William Hall, Chicago-based entrepreneur and former Professor, University of Michigan

"George Siedel details the century-long history of this remarkable, magnificent institution with grace, fidelity and, yes, even love."
—Tim Fort, Eveleigh Professor of Business Ethics, Indiana University

"Siedel masterfully chronicles Ross's founding and evolution while explaining how its faculty, administrators, and alumni have fulfilled the school's enduring mission of building a better world through business."
—Tom Highley, Managing Partner, Cordis Capital Partners

"Reading this book has been a tremendous educational journey for me."
—Brian Wu, Robert G. Rodkey Professor of Business Administration, University of Michigan

"A delightful book honoring the school's 100th anniversary."
—Frank Wilhelme, former Assistant Dean of Development and Alumni Relations, Michigan Ross School of Business

"The [secret] sauce is made from the finest ingredients, the blending of spices is carefully managed, and the process—ever-changing—is difficult to copy."
—Ray Reilly, Professor of Business Administration (retired), University of Michigan

"What a tour de force!"
—Dennis Severance, Accenture Professor of Computer and Information Systems Emeritus, University of Michigan

Contents

About the Author ... i

Introduction ... iii

PART I. MICHIGAN ROSS THEN AND NOW

   Chapter 1. The Birth of Michigan Ross ... 1

   Chapter 2. The Business School During the 1925–26 Academic Year ... 12

   Chapter 3. The Business School at Age Fifty: The 1974–75 Academic Year ... 29

   Chapter 4. The Michigan Ross Centennial: The 2023–24 Academic Year ... 44

PART II. LEGENDARY PROFESSORS

   Chapter 5. William "Bill" Paton: Outstanding Educator of the Century ... 71

   Chapter 6. Paul McCracken: A Modest and Influential Advisor to Eight Presidents ... 84

   Chapter 7. Mary Bromage: Navigating the Shoals of Discrimination ... 103

   Chapter 8. Al Edwards: A "Dean of Inspiration" Arrives After a Student Uprising ... 120

   Chapter 9. CK Prahalad: The World's Most Influential Thinker ... 138

PART III. BEYOND THE MICHIGAN ROSS CAMPUS: ANN ARBOR AND THE UNIVERSITY OF MICHIGAN

    Chapter 10. The Best College Town and a Popular Student Hangout   157

    Chapter 11. Michigan Ross Ties to Athletics Within a World-Renowned University   168

PART IV. THE SECRET SAUCE AT MICHIGAN ROSS

    Chapter 12. The Secret Sauce at Michigan Ross   201

Acknowledgments   221

Notes   223

Figure Credits   237

About the Author

GEORGE J. SIEDEL is the Williamson Family Professor Emeritus of Business Administration and the Thurnau Professor Emeritus of Business Law at the University of Michigan. He completed graduate studies at the University of Michigan and Cambridge University.

Professor Siedel was a Visiting Professor at Stanford University and Harvard University, a Visiting Scholar at Berkeley, and a Parsons Fellow at the University of Sydney. He has been elected a Visiting Fellow at Cambridge University's Wolfson College and a Life Fellow of the Michigan State Bar Foundation. As a Fulbright Scholar in Eastern Europe, he held a Distinguished Chair in the Humanities and Social Sciences.

The author of numerous books and articles, Professor Siedel has received several national research awards (the Hoeber Award, the Ralph Bunche Award, and the Maurer Award) and the University of Michigan's Faculty Recognition Award. In 2018, the Academy of Legal Studies in Business selected Professor Siedel for its Distinguished Career Achievement Award.

Professor Siedel has received many teaching awards, including the Bernard Teaching Leadership Award and the Master of Accounting Program Teaching Excellence Award from the University of Michigan and the Executive Program Professor of the Year Award from a consortium of leading universities.

About the Author

George J. Siedel

Introduction

THIS BOOK ORIGINATED with an email I received on November 12, 2021, from Francine Lafontaine, interim dean at the Ross School of Business at the University of Michigan. She asked me to serve on a small team created to plan a celebration of the business school's centennial anniversary in 2024. The team was co-chaired by Amy Byron-Oilar, the school's chief of staff whom Francine described as "the go-to person for all that is well-organized in the dean's office," and Rajeev Batra, a chaired professor of marketing and leading expert on global branding. Other members of the team were:

- Lynnette Iannace, Director of Events
- Caitlin Johnson, Director of Alumni Engagement
- Jennifer Monaghan, Chief Marketing Officer
- Jim Walsh, a chaired professor of management and organizations and past president of the Academy of Management

As great leaders are inclined to do, Francine assured me that the "amount of work should not be much." Two years and eighteen meetings later, we completed our task. Amy's leadership matched her reputation, and our well-organized meetings were filled with a combination of intense planning and laughter that reflected our respect for each other and dedication to the school. Our work

Introduction

finished, Jennifer, Lynnette, and Caitlin did a remarkable job implementing our recommendations.

Early in our planning, it dawned on me that I have taught at Michigan Ross for fifty of its one hundred years. I served under eight of the school's eleven deans and have taught a diverse range of students from Baby Boomers to Generation Z. Among my colleagues when I arrived at Michigan Ross were two members of the first graduating class in 1926 (one I would often see in the faculty lounge) and four members of the original faculty. My experience as an associate dean at the school provided an administrative perspective. (This experience qualified me to become a member of an association of former associate deans called the Society of St. Sebastian, the long-suffering martyr whose body is pierced with arrows in seventeenth-century paintings.) As a visiting faculty member at other schools (Berkeley, Cambridge, Harvard, and Stanford), I also had an outsider view of the school.

These experiences caused me to think about a question that arose when strategic planning was one of my responsibilities as associate dean: What is the "secret sauce" that has made Michigan Ross one of the world's leading business schools? A starting point in searching for an answer is a history of the school called *Tradition, Vision & Change*, prepared by a team of staff members to mark the 75th anniversary of the school in 1999. This book provides a wonderful 126-page survey of the school's history through the end of the twentieth century but does not address the secret sauce question.

As an undergraduate, my senior thesis focused on social history, sometimes called "history from below." While social history carries a variety of definitions, to Charles Tilly (a prominent history and sociology professor at Michigan), the field emphasizes the role of people's lives in historical change. I decided to use this people-oriented approach to search for the secret sauce.

The result is a book that highlights stories about the people of Ross, often using their own words and occasionally complemented

Introduction

by experiences from my half-century at the school. The book also provides an in-depth, behind-the-scenes perspective on selected topics and extends *Tradition, Vision & Change* by adding the last quarter century, from 1999 to 2024. During this period, the school experienced momentous change driven by disruptive technology and other developments in the business environment.

This Book's Organization

Michigan Ross Then and Now. This book's first four chapters provide a snapshot of the school at three points in time: the mid-1920s, the mid-1970s, and the mid-2020s. Chapter 1 covers the school's birth, emphasizing Dean Edmund Day's negotiations with President Marion Burton and his subsequent efforts to organize the school quickly. Chapter 2 animates the early days of the school by examining a day in the life of beloved professor "Doc" Wolaver, closing with a sad epilogue on the death of his youngest son.

Focusing on the 1974–75 academic year, Chapter 3 surveys the incremental changes occurring during the school's first fifty years. Chapter 4, on the 2023–24 academic year, delves into the significant changes, primarily driven by technology disruption, at the school during its second fifty years, including what happened when the technology crashed at the beginning of the year.

Faculty Legends. Chapters 5–9 focus on five faculty legends: Professors Paton, McCracken, Bromage, Edwards, and Prahalad. Because their accomplishments are well-known, these chapters aim to bring them to life and find the person behind the resume. How did a poor farm boy like Bill Paton become the outstanding educator of the twentieth century? What frustration did Paul McCracken express in his diary on March 14, 1939, when he was twenty-three? How did Mary Bromage react when a Michigan professor told her, "No woman will ever assist me"? What did the principal at his small segregated high school in Key West do to inspire Al Edwards to achieve success? How did CK Prahalad shock executives into action during a weekend retreat at a multinational company? In answering these and other questions, the legendary professors tell their stories in their own words whenever possible.

Town and University. An ingredient that is especially important in the secret sauce at Michigan Ross is its location within a major university that, in turn, is located in one of the best places to live in America. Chapter 10 focuses on the city of Ann Arbor, particularly on a business located a few steps from the school: Casa Dominick's. This popular hangout, the birthplace of one of the world's largest companies, has a business model that raises a perplexing question for all business students. Chapter 11 explores Michigan Ross connections to the University of Michigan, especially the link between the school and athletics.

The Secret Sauce. Chapter 12 describes the secret sauce's key ingredients and explains why it is difficult for other schools to copy them.

The Research Process

I conducted my research at the Bentley Historical Library, which became my home away from home during the summer and fall of 2023. The Bentley is a jewel in the crown of the University of Michigan libraries. Established in 1935, twelve years after the founding of Michigan Ross, the library describes itself as a place "where history lives." It contains 11,000 research collections on the history of the State of Michigan and the University of Michigan.

Conducting research at Bentley felt like going through family boxes in an attic. Sorting through these boxes (over fifty on Paul McCracken alone) was a bittersweet experience—bitter because it brought back fond memories of people long departed and sweet because it enabled me to have conversations with them. I heard their

Introduction

voices as I read their correspondence and other materials untouched by human hands since they were created.

An unexpected treat when conducting research at the Bentley was the discovery that it is a mini-nature preserve. I spotted a flock of wild turkeys on the south side between the Bentley and the Gerald R. Ford Presidential Library. While conducting my research, I could look out a glass wall to the north at a garden that a doe and two fawns occasionally visited. Library staff told me that a buck had rubbed his antlers against the library's brick wall. My favorite character in the garden was a woodchuck nicknamed "General Bentley" by the staff. One day, he peeked into a window by my desk to check how my research was going.

Figure I.1. General Bentley

Introduction

In appreciation for the support provided by the Bentley Historical Library and the career provided by Michigan Ross, I am donating my royalties from this book to both of these outstanding institutions.

Advice for Success

This book is filled with anecdotes about the history of Michigan Ross. These include why founding Dean Day was nicknamed "Rufus" (Chapter 1). The dorm that, at the time the school was founded, provided students with maids, a full-time tailor, and waiters in the dining room (Chapter 2). A comparison of MBA starting salaries with those of associate professors in the mid-1970s (Chapter 3). The unexpected meeting of King (then Prince) Charles with BBA students in 2011 (Chapter 4). The intelligence game that Bill Paton performed at a party that, in all likelihood, no current business school professor in America could master (Chapter 5). Paul McCracken's meeting in Japan with the founder of Toyota, who told Paul that he doubted whether his cars could be successful in America (Chapter 6).

Other anecdotes include Mary Bromage's memo explaining why women on campus who did not eat the crusts on their bread were still entitled to be served toast (Chapter 7). The personal danger experienced by Dean Bond during a student protest (Chapter 8). CK Prahalad's unique solution when dealing with a student who refused to participate on a team (Chapter 9). The presence of vampires at a popular hangout a few steps from the business school (Chapter 10). The BBA student (and later CEO) who was the first New York Giants player to gain 1,000 yards in a season (Chapter 11). What happened when a fire destroyed three MBA students' belongings shortly before exams (Chapter 12).

In addition to these anecdotes, the chapters on legendary professors contain advice for success. Bill Paton, whose teaching was praised by former students who became CEOs of large companies,

Introduction

summarizes his key to business success. The chapter on Paul McCracken reveals the many hours he spent expressing gratitude to others. Mary Bromage provides sage career advice to women that is useful to anyone seeking success. The career of Al Edwards shows how his influence was grounded in his ability to listen to the concerns of others. CK Prahalad's success exemplifies the advice he gave students: "Leadership is having a point of view about the future."

An inscription on the façade of Michigan's Clements Library at Michigan reads: "Tradition fades, but the written word remains forever fresh." I hope the words in this book will remain fresh and prevent the fading of the wonderful traditions at Michigan Ross.

PART I

MICHIGAN ROSS THEN AND NOW

Chapter 1. The Birth of Michigan Ross

Chapter 2. The Business School During the 1925–26 Academic Year

Chapter 3. The Business School at Age Fifty: The 1974–75 Academic Year

Chapter 4. The Michigan Ross Centennial: The 2023–24 Academic Year

Chapter 1

The Birth of Michigan Ross

THE DEAN OF a leading business school has one of the most daunting jobs in academia. During a recent dean search at Michigan Ross, a search firm listed the dean's responsibilities and expectations. Here is a partial list:

- Establish the strategic direction of the school "in the face of changing social, economic, and political landscapes"

- Develop the school's financial strength through fundraising

- Create innovative, interdisciplinary, and global programs that redefine business education

- Provide international visibility for Ross

- Create an environment that promotes excellence in teaching and research

- Recruit, retain, and lead the outstanding faculty and staff necessary to maintain the school's international reputation

- Engage with students to build the "purpose-driven nature of the community"

- Cultivate ties with business leaders and alumni

I. Michigan Ross Then and Now

Given this job description, a dean might be tempted to wistfully recall the school's early days when fifteen faculty members taught the twenty-two students entering its new MBA program, disruptive technology was not present, the terms "trigger warnings" and "cancel culture" were not part of the vocabulary, and improving school rankings and fundraising were not part of the dean's responsibilities.

However, Michigan Ross's founding dean, Edmund Ezra Day, faced his own unusual challenges when planning to launch the school in 1924. He had to prepare a budget, recruit faculty and students, locate classrooms and offices, create a library, develop the curriculum, and publish information about the school. In addition to addressing these challenges as dean, he had teaching responsibilities. A student described a moment in his statistics class when Dean Day "was putting a lot of equations on the board, filling the board, and he turned to us and said, 'I never thought I'd get through that.'" According to the student, "You can't dislike a man like that."

In the school's early days, the dean also handled student relations, sometimes with disappointing results. Consider the sad case of Clara Menger. In a letter dated October 10, 1926, Dean Day advised the university's Graduate School that "Miss Menger was given a 'D' in Economics 175, a course she took some time ago. Last year she covered Economics 176 with a grade of 'B.' In view of the marked improvement in the second course, and the fact that Course 175 is not needed by Miss Menger for credit, I approve Miss Menger's request that the record showing the 'D' in Economics 175 be stricken out." When the Graduate School responded that proof of an injustice was required before a grade could be changed, Dean Day reported to Ms. Menger, "I am sorry to have to write you that fate is against you in that you must carry for the rest of your days the dark grade of 'D' in Economics 175."

1. The Birth of Michigan Ross

Early Days of Business Administration Courses at Michigan

Although it is commonly believed that business courses at the University of Michigan were first offered in 1900, business-related courses were taught much earlier. In the fall of 1882, Economics Professor Henry Carter Adams began teaching a course on the "Principles and Methods of Finance," along with a finance seminar. At the time, no university had an MBA program, and only the University of Pennsylvania had a separate business school for undergraduates, Wharton, which began admitting students in 1881.

Additional business courses were added before the turn of the century. During the 1889–90 academic year, two commercial courses were offered—both on foreign commercial relations. In 1890–91, a course included lectures on commercial crises, and in 1891–92, the course on foreign commercial relations changed its focus to the commercial development of the United States.

By the 1900–01 academic year, the university decided to group existing business courses to meet the career needs of students. As noted in *The Calendar* for that year, the courses aimed "to give a scientific training in the structure and organization of modern industry and commerce and thus enable the student quickly to master the technique of any business career." Additional courses were soon added to the curriculum, including a course in accounting in 1901. Michigan offered what it claimed to be the first university course in marketing in 1902.

The business curriculum soon evolved into a certificate program. According to the 1904–05 *Calendar*, students taking business courses "are entitled to receive, in addition to their diploma, a certificate signed by the President stating the special or professional courses completed in the course in Commerce."

Several students taking these courses became influential academics at other universities. The academics included James Adams (an accounting professor who was chairman of the Economics Department at Brown), Ray Leffler (a finance professor who was chairman of the Economics Department at Dartmouth), Roy Cowin (who taught accounting at Carnegie Tech), and Ross Walker (who taught accounting at Harvard).

Negotiations for the Creation of the Business School

Business courses experienced a surge in enrollment following World War I, causing university President Marion Burton to recognize the need to establish a separate business school. He soon began discussions with Harvard Professor Day about creating the new school. Day's academic credentials included receiving the Rufus Choate Award for scholastic achievement as an undergraduate at Dartmouth, which resulted in his lifelong nickname "Rufus."

Figure 1.1. Edmund Ezra Day

1. The Birth of Michigan Ross

President Burton's discussions came to a head when Day sent him a letter on February 22, 1922, asking for a concrete proposal. Burton responded on March 1, 1922, with an offer letter containing four parts:

1. A position as Professor of Economics and Chairman of the Department of Economics at a salary of $7,500.

2. An assurance that the Board of Regents would "look with favor" if Day recommended creating a business school. Burton noted, "We all agree that the whole problem of business education in American universities is rather acute. We entertain the hope of working out here a plan and an organization which will make a real contribution to the solution of this problem."

3. An assurance that Day would become dean of the new school at a salary of $8,500.

4. A willingness to allow Day to hire two full professors.

In closing his letter, Burton stated, "I am confident that we are offering to you an exceptional opportunity."

Day's reply on March 6, 1922, took exception to this "exceptional opportunity." He had two financial concerns. First, he felt that the salary offer was too low. Objecting to the salary was delicate because he probably realized that a counteroffer would terminate Burton's offer. So, instead of directly asking for a salary of $10,000, he stated, "Unpleasant as I find the subject, I have no course but to speak freely about my future salary.... If it is decided that the University shall have a first-class School of Business Administration, the position of dean of the School may well carry a salary of $10,000."

Day's second financial concern was more general. He had learned that the budget of the Harvard Business School (which already had 500 students and fifteen faculty members) was around $210,000. Given that the new business school at Michigan might be "just as expensive," Day wondered whether the Regents were "hospitable to the development of comprehensive instruction in business administration entailing, as such inevitably will, liberal financial support."

In his reply on March 16, Burton agreed to a salary of $10,000. The budget concern was more difficult for the Board of Regents to address, and Burton noted that "this portion of your letter was read twice at the meeting of the Board." After what was probably considerable debate, Burton crafted this so-called assurance: "I think you may have every assurance that if the work in Business Administration develops and shows real accomplishments that the Board of Regents within its resources will endeavor to provide adequate support."

Burton's letter closed by emphasizing, "I cannot conceive how a more appealing or exceptional opportunity could be offered to a man in his chosen field. In my own mind I am confidently assuming that you will accept." Despite Burton's ambiguous budget assurance, Day accepted the offer and began planning his move to Michigan in 1923.

In the meantime, Day visited Ann Arbor in November 1922 to work on the budget. What else should he do during his visit? Attend a football game, of course. Michigan was undefeated that year and, earlier in the season, played in the dedication game at the Ohio State University stadium, which the Wolverines won 19-0.

On November 9, 1922, economics professor Leo Sharfman wrote a letter to "Dear Day." (Sharfman's later letters began with a warmer "Dear Rufus.") "I wish you would give me the pleasure of being my guest at the Michigan-Wisconsin football game Saturday afternoon. This is our big home game of the year, and the supply of tickets has been exhausted for a long time. It happens, however, that my wife is going east the day before the game, so that I have one of

1. The Birth of Michigan Ross

'the coveted paste-boards' (to use the words of the sport writers) to spare."

Figure 1.2. Both halves of a "paste-board" to the November 18, 1922, game between Michigan and Wisconsin (from the collection of Joe Siedel)

Day responded to "Dear Sharfman" that he could "think of no better way to top off my visit than by witnessing a first-class gridiron contest. I hope I may see my first Michigan victory." Unknown to Day, he would soon be asked to chair a committee that produced the "Day Report." As noted in Chapter 11 of this book, this report created the blueprint for the future of athletics at Michigan and led to the construction of the largest stadium in the United States.

The Birth of a New School

After his arrival in February 1923, Day developed a plan for organizing the School of Business Administration, which he submitted to the Board of Regents on December 14, 1923, on behalf of the Department of Economics. The plan asked the Board to establish a business school that would expand the current business course offerings. Students completing a two-year program would be awarded a Master of Business Administration. The plan called for the opening of the school in September 1924 "with at least a skeleton organization and an offering of its full first-year program."

The plan explained that a new school was necessary because of the professional nature of the instruction. A separate school would enable the development of "highly important contacts with outside business concerns. . . . These contacts are known to be indispensable in the development of satisfactory instruction in Business Administration, as well as in the pursuit of valuable research in the field."

When Day developed his plan, there were two models of business school education. Some schools offered a four-year undergraduate program, while others had created two-year graduate programs focused on professional studies. Day's model was a compromise between the "purely graduate and purely undergraduate types of school." Michigan students would take three years of undergraduate courses followed by two years of professional study, a plan designed to provide graduates with "excellent training for positions of responsibility."

At its meeting on December 20, 1923, the Board of Regents—after approving a proposal to spend $100 to purchase Indian relics and before declining a motion to buy radium—approved the creation of the school effective July 1, 1924. Although continuing his appointment as chairman of the Department of Economics, Professor Day now became Dean Day, with a salary of $10,000.

Dean Day received the school's birth announcement in a letter dated December 24, 1923, from an assistant secretary of the university (a position below that of purchasing agent): "I take pleasure in informing you that at the meeting of the Regents held December 20, the Board approved your recommendations for the organization of the School of Business Administration."

Launching the New School

Dean Day must have received the Christmas Eve letter with a combination of relief and anxiety. While undoubtedly pleased that his plan had been approved, he had only nine months to prepare for the arrival of the first students in September 1924. What courses would be taught, and where would they be offered? Where could he find high-quality faculty and staff? Where would classrooms and faculty offices be located? Would any students be interested in the new program? How could he promote the school to the business community? Who would draft the school's first bulletin?

Undaunted by these challenges, Day immediately kicked into action. On December 29, 1923, one week after the school's birth, a detailed article in *The Detroit News* described the new school. In the article, Dean Day discussed the two key "planks" of the new school's platform. One plank—developing the students' ability to "discover and apply the laws of scientific business management"—was similar to the description of business courses offered earlier by the Department of Economics.

Day's second plank was inspirational. He wanted the new business school to develop students "with broad social vision who will render service to their communities through the agency of their business management." This vision was incorporated into the school's bylaws, stating that the school's instruction would include "the relationship between business leadership and the more general interests of the community."

In the article, Dean Day emphasized that the program of study would be challenging. "To obtain the Master's degree will require long, hard and persistent plugging. Give us but five years and we will turn out a product which we will certify to the business world as satisfactory, sound and capable of the severe tests it has to offer."

Dean Day continued to promote the school during the spring of 1924. At a University Chamber of Commerce "smoker" at the Union, he described the new school's goals and location in Tappan Hall. Other activities on the evening's program included a jiu-jitsu act, a fencing demonstration, and music by a dance orchestra.

By April 1924, planning had advanced to the stage where Dean Day, in an article in the *Michigan Daily*, asked students to leave their names with him if they were interested in enrolling in the new school. In May, students were advised that they could pick up preliminary announcements of the new school at the Department of Economics.

The school's 1924–25 *Bulletin* listed fifteen faculty members, including the dean. Most faculty members were recruited from the Department of Economics (seven) and Harvard (five). The *Bulletin* emphasized the importance of a close connection with the business community for case preparation and business research.

The *Bulletin* also stated that students had to complete an approved program of study to earn an MBA degree. The eight programs of study were Sales Management, Financial Management, Personnel Management, Accounting, Business Statistics, Bank Management, Retail Store Management, and Realty Management. While each program had its own set of courses, all students had to complete a thesis—a requirement that, in the words of two members of the class of 1926, "tried our souls."

First-semester classes began September 23 and ended February 6, after a one-day break for Thanksgiving and a holiday break from December 19 to January 6. Second-semester classes ran from February 9 until commencement on June 15, with one-day breaks for Washington's Birthday and Memorial Day and an eleven-day spring recess. The annual fee for Michigan residents was $85 (for men) and $80 (for women). Out-of-state men paid $110 and women $105.

1. The Birth of Michigan Ross

Twenty-two students enrolled in the new school, creating an attractive faculty-student ratio of 15:22. They registered for classes in the dean's office, where they dropped off a list of the courses they intended to take.

The registration form asked students to state their legal names (forbidding the use of nicknames, pet names, and "any whimsical changes") and their father's occupation. They were "urgently requested" (but not required) to state their church membership or preference. After paying tuition, students were entitled to receive an "Athletic Admission book" from the Director of Outdoor Athletics.

The first class, totaling thirteen students, graduated on June 14, 1926. Following a 7:30 a.m. bugle call and raising of the American flag on the campus, these pioneering MBA students marched with other Michigan graduates to Ferry Field, the venue for football games, for commencement exercises.

His mission accomplished, Dean Day left the University of Michigan in 1928 and later became one of six University of Michigan faculty members to serve as president of Cornell University. On October 5, 1949, twenty-five years after the business school was founded, he returned to Ann Arbor to give a convocation address. Recalling that he "attended its birth" and that the experience of creating a new school was "hectic," he was pleased that current school leaders had continued to "stress the importance of giving to business leadership through professional education a more definite sense of its public obligations."

As noted in later chapters of this book, linking business leadership to the general interests of the community has become a hallmark of the school. The school's mission states: "We must unlock the potential of business by developing powerful ideas, purpose-driven leaders, and a community dedicated to making a positive impact. We are globally-recognized thought leaders who put our ideas into action to tackle some of the world's most important challenges."

Chapter 2

The Business School During the 1925–26 Academic Year

CHAPTERS 2–4 EXAMINE the history of Michigan Ross by focusing on three academic years. This chapter concentrates on the 1925–26 academic year, which culminated in the graduation of the school's first class. After discussing the university's parental role, the chapter features a day in the life of a professor at the time.

Chapter 3 moves to the 1974–75 academic year, when the business school celebrated its 50th anniversary. Chapter 4 focuses on 2023–24, the school's 100th academic year.

The Parental Role of the University of Michigan When the Business School Was Founded

During the 1920s, students balanced newfound freedom with institutional regulations. They reveled in their independence, enjoying roller skating, driving cars, listening to radios, and going to the movies. As described by Howard Peckham in *The Making of the University of Michigan 1817–1992*, "this was the era of the flapper—the coed with bobbed hair, painted face, a falling waist line, and rolled stockings." Her escort, on the other hand, "sported sideburns, pomaded hair, a hat of improbable convolutions, bellbottom trousers, and 'loud' socks." They shared a love for dancing, particularly the Charleston, which epitomized the era's spirit.

2. The 1925–26 Academic Year

However, students were also subject to governmental and university regulations. Congress prohibited the sale of alcohol when passing the Volstead Act in 1919. The university had its own set of restrictions acting *in loco parentis*—in place of the students' parents. Here are examples of the parental regulations quoted from the 1924–25 *Catalogue and Register*.

> **Students' Physical Welfare.** [A] sound, vigorous, harmoniously developed, and active physique is a most important essential to the success of the student, not only while he is in the University, but later in his life. . . .
>
> - Every [male] student is measured and furnished with an anthropometric chart, which affords a comparison of his own measurements with those of the average student and reveals for correction any abnormality that may be present. . . . [During required physical training,] special attention is given to arm and chest exercises, since the development of these parts of the body is below normal in a great majority of the men who come to college.
>
> - [In required courses for women], attention is given to the correction of faulty posture and any deformity that may be benefited by intelligent exercise. . . . A regulation costume of white blouse, black bloomers, and black gymnasium shoes is required.
>
> - [Through an intramural program, students develop] a knowledge and love of many sports, so that they may keep up their spirit after the college life is over. [Intramural sports included speedball, rifle shooting, bowling, handball, fencing, horseshoe pitching, and a mysterious sport called playground ball.]
>
> - [A Board in Control supervised intercollegiate athletics] to foster the spirit of honor and gentlemanliness in athletics, to

suppress evil tendencies, and to see that play shall not encroach too much upon the claims of work.

University Health Service. [UHS was supposed to protect] the physically sound student from communicable diseases that continually creep into the University. This is done through early detection and isolation of all cases of communicable disease—tuberculosis, typhoid fever, smallpox, scarlet fever, mumps, measles, diphtheria, etc. [UHS also provides correction] of defects, advice, and treatment to all subnormals. . . . ["Subnormal" is not defined.]

Students are urged to select good rooms, with special attention to hygienic conditions. All rooms should be easily ventilated, kept at about 65 degrees temperature, separate for study and sleep, and should have single beds and individual drinking cups. Examination of sputum will be made at the Health Service laboratory. . . .

Living Accommodations. There are no dormitories for men and no commons connected with the University, the men all rooming and boarding in private houses. . . . Since the University believes that men and women should room in separate houses, all undergraduate women in the University, except those living at home, are required to live in the Halls of Residence, Sorority Houses, or University Houses.

Attendance and Discipline. [The university] cannot . . . be the patron of idleness or dissipation. Its crowded classes have no room except for those who assiduously pursue the studies of their choice and are willing to be governed in their conduct by the rules of propriety.

Student Self Help. [The university maintains] an employment bureau for men students. . . . A large number of students earn their board by either waiting on table or washing dishes at boarding houses and fraternities, and many pay for their rooms by taking care of furnaces, cleaning walks, washing windows, etc.

Fees and Expenses. The annual expenses of students, including [tuition, room, board, clothing and incidentals] are on the average, somewhat over six hundred dollars.

Did universities have the legal right to impose these restrictions on students? The Michigan Supreme Court addressed this question in 1924, the year the business school was founded. Alice Tanton, eighteen, filed a lawsuit challenging her expulsion from Michigan State Normal College (now Eastern Michigan University). According to the court, she "had become addicted to the smoking of cigarettes, . . . smoked cigarettes on the public streets of Ypsilanti, . . . [and] rode around the streets of Ypsilanti in an automobile seated on the lap of a young man."

A trial court decided that this conduct justified the college's refusal to readmit Alice. On appeal, the Michigan Supreme Court agreed. The court noted that the trial court had correctly rejected evidence that male students and professors also smoked. The court further observed that it is up to the school, not the courts, to develop disciplinary regulations.

After the dean of women had displayed "a motherly interest in her" and attempted to get her "out of the rut she was traveling in," Alice had aired a "defiance of discipline in the public press." This defiance alone, the court concluded, "was sufficient grounds for refusing her admission." Apparently, the parental rights of the college had priority over the rights of Alice's mother, who had joined her as a plaintiff in the case.

I. Michigan Ross Then and Now

A Day in the Life of a Business School Professor

Earl S. Wolaver, affectionately known as "Doc," was a beloved professor in the early years of the business school. A graduate of the University of Michigan undergraduate program and law school, he joined the faculty in 1920. Doc lived at 1310 Hill Street in a neocolonial Georgian revival house. A chemistry professor built the house in 1890 and sold it in 1901 to a widow, Margaret Lydecker. She operated a boarding house known for the "best food in Ann Arbor." After her daughter, also named Margaret, married Doc, they raised their family in the house.

When Doc began teaching at the new business school, students took seven required courses during the first year (Marketing Principles, Financial Principles, Production Management, Managerial Organization and Control, Sales Management, Financial Management, and Personnel Management) and four required courses in the second year (Business Policy I and II, Business Law, and Business Forecasting and Budgeting). They also had to complete foundational accounting, economics, and statistics courses before admission.

Figure 2.1. Earl "Doc" Wolaver, third row down, second from right

2. The 1925–26 Academic Year

Doc taught the required Business Law course. Although based on Doc's life and the early history of the business school, the following account uses historical fiction to bring the facts to life and recreate a day in his life.

6:30–7:15 a.m. On Monday, October 12, 1925, thirty-nine-year-old Doc starts his day with breakfast early in the morning before his wife Margaret and five-year-old son John awaken. Margaret is expecting the couple's second child in late November. As he sips his coffee, Doc thinks about the good news recently reported in newspapers. As a result of the Locarno treaty negotiations in Switzerland, Germany will never again declare war on other European countries. Doc feels relieved that his children will never experience a world war like the Great War that ended seven years ago.

7:15–7:30 a.m. After breakfast, Doc walks to his office in Tappan Hall. Dressed in a three-piece suit, he wears an overcoat on this unusually chilly day in Ann Arbor, with a high temperature in the mid-50s. Fall is his favorite time of year, when the leaves on the tree-lined streets in Ann Arbor morph from green to a mixture of red, yellow, and orange colors.

Doc first walks west on Hill Street past several fraternity houses to East University, a street that was originally the eastern border of campus. He then proceeds north on East University to South University (the original southern border), past the new University High School that opened in 1924. Turning left on South University, he passes West Engineering (with its famous arch designed to allow pedestrians to use a preexisting diagonal walk through campus) to his favorite building on campus, the Clements Library. Designed by famed architect Albert Kahn in Italian Renaissance style, the library opened in 1923.

Doc then passes the university president's house, one of four houses built initially for university faculty in 1837. Since then, university presidents have occupied the house, although it occasionally served other purposes, such as headquarters for the Red Cross during the recent Great War.

Opposite the Clements Library and the president's house stands the English Gothic-style Martha Cook Residence Hall, donated by New York City attorney William Cook in honor of his mother—on the condition that the university provide free heat, light, and power. Cook also donated the new Law School Lawyers Club and dorm across the street from Martha Cook. The facility provides first-class services for law students, including maids, a full-time tailor, and waiters in the dining room.

Turning down a path to the right, Doc's twelve-minute walk ends at Tappan Hall. Constructed in 1894, the building is shared by education and business school professors, who call it the "Little Red Schoolhouse."

Figure 2.2. Tappan Hall

2. The 1925–26 Academic Year

7:30–10:45 a.m. After entering the building, Doc goes to his office in the basement near the boiler room, where he prepares for today's classes. He first reviews his lecture notes for an 11:00 a.m. Department of Economics course on the legal framework of commercial transactions. (After creation of the business school, Economics continued to offer business administration courses until the 1927–28 academic year.) He is well prepared for this course, having taught it for several years. So, he focuses most of his preparation on the new MBA course he will teach at 2 p.m.

The new course covers the legal aspects of enterprise organization, including principal-agent relations, partnerships, and corporations. Today, Doc plans to focus on a question related to shareholder primacy theory: Must business leaders prioritize the interests of shareholders over other stakeholders—or will courts refuse to interfere with business decisions under the so-called "business judgment rule"?

The Michigan Supreme Court addressed this issue in a leading case six years earlier (in 1919) involving a company not far from the university: Henry Ford's motor company. Two shareholders—the Dodge brothers—sued the company, claiming it should distribute company profits through a hefty dividend. Henry Ford disagreed and wanted to reinvest the profits into the business. He publicly stated, "I do not believe we should make such an awful profit on our cars. A reasonable profit is right, but not too much. So it has been my policy to force the price of the car down as fast as production would permit and give the benefits to users and laborers."

When asked in court about the purpose of the Ford Motor Company, Ford responded: "Organized to do as much good as we can, everywhere, for everybody concerned." The case was ideal for sparking class discussion of the relationship between business and community interests. Dean Day emphasized the importance of this relationship when the new business school was created the previous year.

In preparing for class, Doc refers to the leading textbooks of the time. He especially likes *Law and Business* by William Spencer, a business law professor and business school dean at the University of Chicago, and *The Law in Business* by Lincoln Schaub and Nathan Isaacs, two business law professors at Harvard Business School.

After his class preparation, Doc reviews his research on land use regulation and planning. In the early years of the twentieth century, large cities such as Los Angeles and New York City enacted zoning laws, and Ann Arbor followed suit with its first zoning ordinance in 1923. Business leaders now needed guidance to understand these laws. To complicate matters, courts had to decide whether the new laws were constitutional. Doc plans to address these concerns in an article and to incorporate his research into a course on Real Estate Law that he will teach next semester.

10:45 a.m.–1:00 p.m. Doc walks to a classroom in the newly completed Angell Hall, where he will teach his Department of Economics course. Before entering the building, he pauses to read the inspiring quotation from the Ordinance of 1787 on the façade: "Religion, morality, and knowledge, being necessary to good government and the happiness of mankind, schools and the means of education shall forever be encouraged." He hopes that his and other courses in the new business school will enable students to leave the university with the combination of knowledge and morality necessary to become successful business leaders.

When class ends at noon, Doc heads to one of his favorite places on campus, the magnificent Michigan Union, which opened six years before in 1919. As he enters the front door, he thinks of the injustice that women cannot use that door and must enter from a side door called the "ladies" entrance. He proceeds to the basement, where he eats lunch in the Tap-Room, a cafeteria near a large swimming pool that just opened in the Union.

2. The 1925–26 Academic Year

1:00–2:00 p.m. Doc returns to his office in Tappan Hall. On entering the building, he smells cigar smoke, which indicates that his colleague Clarence Yoakum is in his office. Yoakum especially enjoys smoking cigar stubs in his pipe. In his office, Doc completes a last-minute review of his notes for the upcoming MBA course.

2:00–3:00 p.m. Upon entering the classroom after climbing two flights of stairs, Doc is reminded of the students' diverse backgrounds. The class includes thirteen students who are on track to become the first graduates of the business school the following spring. In a *Dividend* article on "Ann Arbor and the Business School in the Twenties" (Fall 1971), two of these students, Jim Waterman and Maynard Phelps, described their classmates: "There were two Chinese; two Blacks, one of whom later received a PhD from Harvard; one Pole; one Greek and six miscellaneous Americans of Dutch, Swedish and English ancestry." All students are well dressed (the men wearing suits and ties). Two of them brought roller skates to the classroom.

The students are well prepared for class discussion and almost evenly divided over whether shareholders should have primacy over other stakeholders. They understand that debates like this will not end in the classroom because, later in life, they will face similar disagreements when making decisions allowed by the Business Judgment Rule.

Doc notices that Phelps and Waterman (who room together on South University Avenue) are especially active in the debate and present sophisticated arguments. The other students in class write down their comments. He observes this phenomenon in other courses and has concluded that the ability of certain students to co-create the educational experience by inspiring their already bright peers to greater achievement is a notable aspect of a Michigan education.

3:00–4:00 p.m. Doc meets with several students in his office to continue discussing the *Dodge* case. Because the class is small, he

21

I. Michigan Ross Then and Now

feels close to the students and asks them about their weekend. They enjoyed watching Michigan beat Indiana 63-0 on Saturday at Ferry Field. It was Michigan's worst defeat of a Big Ten opponent since 1902 (when the Wolverines beat Iowa 107-0 and Ohio State 86-0). Quarterback Benny Friedman led an aerial attack by completing nine passes, and sophomore Benny Oosterbaan was outstanding on offense and defense.

Three students mentioned attending the opening of a spectacular new movie, Cecil B. De Mille's *The Ten Commandments*. They were amazed by a scene where the Red Sea parted for the passing of the Israelites and then closed to destroy Pharaoh's army. The music played by the Arcade Symphonic Combination during the film was superb and well worth the higher-than-usual price of fifty cents for admission. They discussed with Doc their belief that companies would soon produce talking pictures.

4:00–5:00 p.m. After the students leave, Doc prepares for a class later in the week, where the main topic will be piercing the corporate veil. He will emphasize that this is a critical topic for business leaders, who need to understand when their decisions might cause them to lose the protection from personal liability provided by corporations.

Doc also thinks about his conversation with the students. He is grateful they wanted to talk about football and a movie instead of the murder that had dominated their discussions a year ago. On September 10, 1924, two weeks before the first classes started at the new business school, two teenagers were sentenced to life in prison for committing what was called the crime of the century. The crime had several links to the University of Michigan. One of the teenagers, Richard Loeb, graduated from the University of Michigan in 1923 at age seventeen—the youngest graduate ever. The other teenager, Nathan Leopold, attended Michigan before transferring to the University of Chicago, where he graduated the same year at age

2. The 1925–26 Academic Year

eighteen. In the fall of 1923, Leopold and Loeb returned to Ann Arbor, where they robbed Loeb's old fraternity, the Zeta Beta Tau house.

Leopold and Loeb also talked about killing one of Loeb's fraternity brothers but eventually murdered his fourteen-year-old neighbor, Bobby Franks, in an attempt to commit a perfect crime. They used a typewriter stolen from the fraternity to type a ransom note, and this turned out to be critical evidence linking them to the crime. After they confessed, attorney Clarence Darrow, who attended the Michigan Law School, successfully argued that they should not be hanged but, instead, should spend life in prison. The judge agreed.

5:00–5:30 p.m. At 5:00 p.m., Doc leaves Tappan Hall. On his way out, he stops to talk with Doris Egley, the school's new librarian. She tells him the library will house around 300 books when it opens in a few weeks.

Doc's trip home takes him through the Diag, where he walks past the Tappan Oak, a magnificent tree over 150 years old. The oak is surrounded by maple trees that provide a spectacular palette of fall colors. Encouraged by a young professor, Andrew Dickson White, students planted the maples in 1858 to honor the university's first president, Henry Tappan. White left the university near the end of the Civil War, and in 1865, he co-founded Cornell University, where he served as the first president.

5:30–10:00 p.m. Doc arrives home. After dinner with Margaret and their son John, they listen to the WCX/WJR radio station. They especially enjoy "The Jewett Jesters" and the blind singer Harold Kean, known as "The Sunshine Boy."

Doc closes out the day by reading a few Robert Frost poems. Frost is returning to campus this semester as a visiting fellow for the third time. During an earlier visit, he met with students to critique their poems in a professor's house on Olivia Avenue, around the corner from where Doc lives. Frost recently won a Pulitzer Prize for his poetry collection *New Hampshire*, which he dedicated to Michigan. Doc especially enjoys a poem in the collection called "Stopping by Woods on a Snowy Evening."

Epilogue

Four members of the first class who graduated in 1926 earned PhDs. The two students who led the discussion in Doc's class, Phelps and Waterman, were co-valedictorians and later became professors at Michigan. In 1930, Waterman authored the first case published by the school's Bureau of Business Research, "The Dey Manufacturing Company."

The 1926 class included the first female business school graduate, Sih Eu-yang Chen. After graduation, she returned home to China, where she married Chungshen Shen, a PhD graduate of Columbia. She worked as an accountant and as a professor at Shanghai College while raising five daughters. The family eventually moved to Hong Kong and then to Berkeley.

In their *Dividend* article, mentioned earlier, Waterman and Phelps noted that one of their classmates "went into banking, two into finance, three into general management, two into government jobs, and two into marketing." In 1935, Dean Clare Griffin sent a salary report to alumni, indicating that the monthly average starting salary for the class of 1926 was $154. After yearly increases to 1930, when it reached $331, the average salary dropped to $232 during the Depression years of 1932–33 before rebounding to $319 in 1935.

Henry Ford, featured in Doc's class discussion, joined the first business school graduates at the 1926 commencement, where he received an honorary degree. He later purchased the Ann Arbor house where Robert Frost lived and moved it to Greenfield Village (a historic village just outside of Detroit and top tourist attraction in Michigan). Ford must have squirmed on the platform while listening to the commencement speaker, Sir Frederick Whyte, discussing

2. The 1925–26 Academic Year

mass production. "It is an era of mass production in motor cars and safety pins; aye, even in men and opinion. And there, in these last few words, lies its greatest danger. The individual man and woman of today is subjected to a pressure which seeks to produce a standard shape, a conformity to certain conventions which is the enemy of individuality."

The football team that students discussed in Doc's office was among the best in Michigan history. The team was undefeated except for a 3-2 loss to Northwestern—the only points scored by a Michigan opponent all season. The team, along with Alabama, ranked second in the country behind Dartmouth.

After talking with students, Doc had thought about what was called the crime of the century. The two teenagers who committed the crime, Leopold and Loeb, were sentenced to life in prison. Leopold was released in 1958 after serving thirty-three years. Loeb died in 1936 at age thirty after a fellow prisoner stabbed him. His Michigan alumni card reads: "Sentenced to Joliet Penitentiary for life. Sept. 10-1924. d. at Joliet, Ill. Jan. 28, 1936; aged 30. Buried at Chicago, Ill."

By 2021, the magnificent Tappan Oak that Doc walked past on his way home from school was diseased and had to be removed. A few years earlier, an undergraduate had planted acorns from the tree that grew into saplings. He gave one of them to the university.

Doc Wolaver died after a heart attack on June 30, 1950, at age 63. *The New York Times* reported that he was an expert on business law and trade barriers in interstate commerce and served for two years as president of what is today the Academy of Legal Studies in Business. (The Academy was founded in 1924, the same year as the Michigan business school, and Doc was the fourth president.)

The faculty meeting minutes on September 26, 1950, provided this warm remembrance:

Since the founding of the School of Business Administration in

I. Michigan Ross Then and Now

1924, the School, its faculty, its students and alumni enjoyed and profited by the wisdom, kindliness and friendship of Professor Earl S. Wolaver. His death in June, 1950, was a loss not only to those who had the privilege of knowing and associating with "Doc" during the years of his loyal interest in all phases of School and University affairs, but also to those of future generations who will be denied that privilege.

The faculty of the School finds it difficult and strange to start a new academic year without his presence. It wishes hereby to express its feeling of loss and at the same time to recognize the lasting contribution that Professor Wolaver made in the councils of the faculty. Not only the School of Business Administration but also the University of Michigan as a whole will long continue to benefit from his influence.

Over breakfast on October 12, 1925, Doc had felt assured that there would never be another world war because of the Locarno Treaty. Eleven years later, Hitler repudiated Locarno when he sent troops into the Rhineland. Doc's second son, David, born in November 1925, was inducted into the Army as a teenager. Here are excerpts from a letter dated May 26, 1943, to his girlfriend Dotty, describing his basic training experiences.

Dearest Dotty,

I finally received two of your letters tonight at mail call, and you can bet that I was the happiest guy there. I thought maybe something had gone wrong at home, but I was relieved greatly when I saw the letters were from you.

I remember you said that you might possibly receive a "D" in biology. I have $50 a month until the duration, that I would bet that you receive either an "A" or "B." If you want to take that bet just let me know. By the way, the best of luck on your exams.

2. The 1925–26 Academic Year

Today was one of the roughest days in my life. It was one that we have all been waiting for. We went through a "blitz course." The boys in our platoon saw some men that went through it in the morning, and they were so dirty and bruised up, they scared the daylights out of us before we even started. But in the afternoon we started for the course. Just as we were about to start, down came the rain. It was terrible.

In the first place, the "blitz course" is supposed to test the soldier under actual combat conditions. It was actual conditions alright, because there were dud bombs, machine gun bullets, and everything else, whizzing over our heads. We were given hand grenades and, of course, we had our rifles & bayonets. We had to cross on slippery logs over canyons that had barbed wire at the bottom, crawl thru trenches on our stomach, blow up machine guns, nest, jab dummies that surprised us and everything else you can think of.

Bombs exploded at our feet and we really had to be alert in order to keep from being hurt. Some boys were badly hurt, but I managed the course in good shape. After this was over I went and stepped into the shower with all my clothes on; this also included my rifle. After I was somewhat clean, I took a brush and scrubbed for twenty-five minutes before anything looked reasonably clean. Really I can't begin to describe here, what went on this afternoon.

But enough for that. After mail call tonight, I was just getting ready to take in a show. Then the worst happened. I was put on K.P. for tonight. I peeled so many potatoes, I will dream about them all night. Anyway, Dotty, I will be in good practice when you become my wife, and I can peel all the potatoes in record time.

I. Michigan Ross Then and Now

I read part of your letter to some of the boys. The part about salt peter. They laughed until they were sick. Don't worry about what they might think, because they like to hear things like that.

I am going to draw this to a close now, for I have to shave and get to bed.

I love you more than I can ever write down on paper, but I hope you believe me because that came from the bottom of my heart.

I really have to close this now, so I will see you in my dreams.

All the love, darling,

Dave

After basic training, while still a teenager, David was sent overseas, where he fought in the North African and Italian campaigns. According to an obituary in *The Michigan Alumnus* (April 14, 1945), he was awarded the Combat Infantry Badge for his work at Anzio beach (the highest award a soldier in the infantry can receive), fought in the battles at Casino and Cisterno, and was one of the first Americans to enter Rome. He was nineteen when he was killed in action on January 15, 1945. David is buried at the American Cemetery in Lorraine, France. After his death, his beloved Dotty married, and her husband donated David's letter to the Bentley Historical Library after she died in 2009.

By the time Margaret died in 1975, John, the Wolavers' other son, had also passed away. Her will established an endowment of $241,056 in honor of David to aid "needy and deserving students" at the business school. The will also created an identical endowment to honor John, a Michigan School of Music faculty member, to aid music students.

Chapter 3

The Business School at Age Fifty: The 1974–75 Academic Year

DURING THE 1974–75 academic year, when the Michigan business school celebrated its 50th birthday, classes began on September 6, 1974. Four weeks earlier to the day, Richard Nixon became the only president to resign from office, and Gerald Ford was sworn in as the 38th president. President Ford graduated in 1935 from Michigan, where he was football team captain. After graduation, he attended Yale Law School instead of accepting offers from the Chicago Bears and Green Bay Packers to play professional football.

Football was in the news on the front page of the September 6 edition of the *Michigan Daily*. An article noted that students began pitching tents five days earlier outside Yost Field House, where they waited in line for football tickets. The football team had been undefeated the prior year, with only a tie with Ohio State to mar the record.

Another *Daily* article predicted that "Michigan again this year will likely go undefeated into its November 23 showdown with Ohio State." Undefeated Michigan lost that game to once-beaten Ohio State 12-10 when Michigan's kicker missed a thirty-seven-yard field goal with eighteen seconds remaining. Despite Michigan's combined 20-1-1 record over the two seasons, the team did not play in a bowl game in either season.

My arrival on campus that fall at age twenty-nine as an assistant professor was a humbling experience, as my cohort of new professors included several colleagues destined for distinguished careers:

- Statistics professor Andy Andrews became a legendary teacher at the business school. The Andy Andrews Distinguished Faculty Service Award was created in his honor.

- Accounting professor Paul Danos taught at the school for two decades before serving another two decades as dean at Dartmouth's Tuck School of Business.

- Business administration professor Al Edwards, whose career is described in Chapter 8, arrived at the business school as the Director of the Division of Business Research following a successful career in government.

- Management science professor Alan Merten later served as dean of the business schools at the University of Florida and Cornell and president of George Mason University for sixteen years.

- Organizational behavior professor Joe White held leadership positions as dean of the business school, interim president of the University of Michigan, and president of the University of Illinois.

Teaching During the 1974–75 Academic Year

During the 1974 Fall Term, I taught three sections of the required business law course. The course introduced students to the legal system, emphasizing the contractual agreements that form the basis for business relationships. The course also covered the fiduciary duties and other legal responsibilities of principals and agents.

3. The Business School at Age Fifty: 1974–75

Route to School. Like Doc Wolaver fifty years earlier, I began my day by walking to the business school, although by a different route. I lived with my family in a small Cape Cod on a stretch of Vinewood Boulevard between Geddes Avenue and Avon Road, across the street from a house owned by theater professor Claribel Halstead. Once a star on Broadway, as a professor she encouraged Michigan premed student (and later voice of Darth Vader) James Earl Jones to become an actor. Legendary Michigan football coach Fielding Yost lived on a hill behind Professor Halstead's house before he passed away in 1946.

My walk to school took me past the homes of my neighbors Bob Forman, longtime director of the Michigan Alumni Association, and Truman Tibbals. Truman had purchased the iconic Drake's Sandwich Shop in 1933, nine years after the business school was founded. Walking past his house, I often thought of him heading to work every morning at 3:30 a.m., age sixty-six and partially blind, to cook bacon for sandwiches sold at Drake's.

Mary Bromage, portrayed in Chapter 7, lived a few houses down the street from Truman. At the end of the street was a home that Tom Harmon (Michigan's first Heisman Trophy winner) built for his parents, using earnings from a Columbia Pictures movie he starred in called *Harmon of Michigan*.

My main challenge when walking to school during early morning hours was the presence of skunks. I occasionally encountered one pair who refused to yield the right of way as they walked down the sidewalk toward me.

Class Preparation. At school, my preparation for class was not unlike the way Doc Wolaver prepared for class. I wrote the course syllabus by hand. After administrative assistants (then called secretaries and today nicknamed "admins") did their best to decipher my handwriting and type the syllabus, I corrected the first draft before they typed the final version.

We used this same process for hundreds of recommendation letters and for my book and article manuscripts. I am indebted to outstanding admins like Linda Gorlitz and Shelly Whitmer, who were adept at anticipating my course preparation, scheduling, and research needs.

In the Classroom. I used formal names when calling on students in class—for example, Mr. Jones, Miss (before Ms. became common) Smith—and students called me Professor Siedel. Like other professors in 1974, I wore a suit and tie, similar to the dress when the school was founded.

Student dress in the post-1960s era changed dramatically. Apart from students dressed for job interviews, faded jeans and T-shirts were common. Their demeanor was also more informal. For instance, one student often leaned back in her chair with her feet on the desk.

As Doc Wolaver had observed fifty years earlier, I noticed that certain students at Michigan set the tone for the class when analyzing a problem or raising a question. For example, during one of my first classes, when covering the ability of a business to assign contract rights, a student I'll call "Bill Smith" ("Mr. Smith") asked a sophisticated question. I noticed that other students in the class—probably all "A" students in high school—sat up straighter in their seats as they became engaged in thinking about the problem.

I didn't have a ready answer to Bill's question, but I quickly developed a strategy that proved helpful throughout my career: I asked "Mr. Smith" how *he* would answer the question. When he hesitated, I candidly admitted that I wasn't sure of the answer but would provide an analysis during the next class (which I did). Several years later, I connected with "Bill" and discovered that he graduated near the top of his class from Harvard Law School and was a partner in a large law firm.

3. The Business School at Age Fifty: 1974–75

Links to the Past. Some of my faculty colleagues in 1974 were linked to the Wolaver era. Four surviving faculty members from the school's opening in 1924 were listed in the faculty directory (Olin Blackett, Clare Griffin, Bill Paton, and Margaret Tracy), along with two students from the first graduating class who became faculty members (Maynard Phelps and Jim Waterman). Although they were all retired, I occasionally saw Maynard (then age seventy-six) and Bill (age eighty-five) in the faculty lounge or hallway. Doc Wolaver's wife, Margaret, aged ninety, still lived in Ann Arbor.

Changes at the Business School over the First Fifty Years

While in 1974 there were similarities to the past, the school had undergone several incremental changes over the previous fifty years. Here are some examples.

Degree Programs. In the mid-1920s, the business school offered only the full-time MBA program. By 1974, students could complete the program by taking evening courses. The school also added a PhD program, which produced its first graduate in 1935.

The school started a Bachelor of Business Administration (BBA) degree program in 1942 to meet the needs created by World War II. The program had a slow start, with sixty-two students registered in 1943 (along with six MBA students), but by 1949, the post-war total enrollment surged to 1,249. From the school's initial enrollment of twenty-two MBA students in 1924, the combined BBA, MBA, and PhD enrollments had grown to 1,629 during Fall Term of 1974.

Research and Ties to the Business Community. The business school's bylaws, adopted after its founding in 1924, state that the school would "seek by every means to encourage that co-operation between the school and business concerns which is necessary to the development of professional training in the field of business."

I. MICHIGAN ROSS THEN AND NOW

According to the bylaws, one means of cooperation was through research designed to assist "in the solution of current problems of modern business."

Faculty research during the school's first fifty years significantly impacted businesses, government, and management education. For instance, Bill Paton, featured in Chapter 5, conducted research that shaped the accounting profession. Paul McCracken (Chapter 6) served as research director for the Federal Reserve Bank in Minneapolis before joining the faculty. His research skills immensely impacted public policy when advising eight presidents.

Other faculty members counseled federal agencies and commissions, and they served on boards of directors and as expert witnesses. Still others became leaders in creating fields such as international marketing, new product development, and healthcare law. In 1936, Professor Charles Jamison proposed the creation of the Academy of Management, which today is the leading association for management and organization scholars with 18,000 members globally. Professor Tom Schriber developed and led a program that helped business school faculty from around the country understand how to use a new tool—the computer—in their teaching and research.

Executive education programs provided another form of cooperation between the business school and the business community espoused by Dean Day. Especially notable were three four-week programs—for bankers, public utility executives, and general managers—that originated in the early 1950s and were thriving by the 1970s. The school also offered over 200 shorter management seminars on topics like management by objectives.

Faculty. By the mid-1970s, the faculty had increased from the original fifteen members to sixty-two. The salaries of full professors ranged from $19,000 to $33,000, except for Paul McCracken (profiled in Chapter 6), whose salary was $39,000. The one female full professor, Mary Bromage (see Chapter 7), received the second

3. The Business School at Age Fifty: 1974–75

lowest salary. Associate professor salaries ranged from $16,200 to $19,200, and assistant professors from $13,700 to $15,930. As a result of the large student enrollments, many professors taught overload courses for extra pay.

Grading of Students and Faculty. In the early years of the business school, an "A" grade was difficult to achieve. For example, in 1933–34, 11 percent of the MBA grades were "A," 38 percent were "B," and 40 percent were "C." By Fall Term 1974, grade inflation was underway. Forty-three percent of MBA students (who by then needed a "B" average to graduate) received grades in the "A" range, and 50 percent received "B+" or "B."

By 1974, grading had become a two-way street, as students graded professors at the end of each semester. Their evaluations were reported to the Dean's Office for use in promotion and tenure decisions, annual salary adjustments, and providing advice to faculty who received low assessments. Although the evaluations were not designed for this purpose, students used them when selecting courses. I discovered this during my second week of teaching when several of my students switched to a section taught by a colleague who ranked high on a list of professors with outstanding evaluations that the student newspaper had just published.

The comments on my evaluations provided helpful suggestions when I started my teaching career at the business school. However, I was unsure how to react when I received this type of comment: "I learned more in your course and received a lower grade than any other." Other comments caused mild disappointment, especially about my selection of ties.

Facilities. Business students initially took classes in Tappan Hall (the so-called "Little Red Schoolhouse"). An article in *Michigan Tradesman* (August 30, 1950) described their experience:

> [T]he Business Administration student at Michigan often had his

classes in rooms that were small and crowded. He sat in a row with half a dozen other students on hard benches, taking his notes on the overgrown right arm of his seat (about the size and shape of a tennis racquet). The room was either too hot or too cold, and usually not well ventilated. Its blackboards shone with a dull luster that made it difficult to read what was written on them; its lights glared and cast shadow; its radiators pounded; its pipes leaked. The student's coat became one of a pile on a window sill; his books lay on the floor beneath his feet.

Classrooms changed for the better in 1948 when the school relocated to a $2.5 million structure at the intersection of Tappan and Monroe Streets. *The Michigan Alumnus* (March 27, 1948) touted the building as "the finest in the world." The structure was nicknamed "The Tower," referring to its nine-story tower sandwiched between two three-story wings. Like Wayne Tower in Batman's Gotham City, the building dominated the landscape of Ann Arbor. A deck on the ninth floor provided an excellent area for viewing July 4 fireworks with my family.

Figure 3.1. The Tower

3. The Business School at Age Fifty: 1974–75

The new building included classrooms, administrative and faculty offices, laboratories, and lounges for students and faculty. By 1948, the library had grown from its original 300 volumes to 30,000, housed in a room that could seat 350 at a time. Rules for the library warned students that "No smoking is allowed. The student lounge is available for that purpose."

At the cornerstone-laying ceremony for the new building on May 24, 1947, university provost James Adams reminded the audience of the "larger purposes for which this School exists." Echoing the goals expressed by the founding dean, he emphasized the university's desire to help students "appreciate the social responsibilities which attach to the business enterprise in any society."

The business school's rapid growth later resulted in construction of Assembly Hall, dedicated in 1972. Funded by private contributions, the addition housed executive education faculty and staff.

During the 1974 Fall Term, I taught my courses in one of the school's two 200-seat classrooms—long, narrow-tiered rooms reminiscent of an airport runway. Students entered from the back of the classroom, where there were coatracks and a place for their books. I entered through a door at the front of the room and taught while standing on a platform. A small room behind me served as a staging area. Unlike the early years at the business school, students sat at tables in comfortable, padded chairs.

Recalling the frightening experience of teaching my first class there on the morning of September 6, 1974, brings to mind a comment in the forward to the book *Education for Judgment* (1991): "[E]xposing one's knowledge, personality, and ego to the scrutiny of others in public is not easy work under the best of circumstances."

Students. Most students in my 1974–75 courses graduated in 1976. A report on the class of 1976 indicated that the median age for MBA graduates was twenty-five, 40 percent were married, 14 percent were women, and 4 percent represented minority groups. Two-thirds of the class were from eight states: Michigan, Illinois, New York, Ohio, Indiana, Connecticut, Massachusetts, and California. My students followed the general pattern of the time in that they were mainly Caucasian males and much less diverse than the first students fifty years earlier and the students enrolled fifty years later.

Forty percent of the students accepted jobs in finance, 19 percent in consulting, 17 percent in accounting, 11 percent in marketing, and 9 percent in computer/management science. The average starting salary was $17,800—the middle of the salary range for the business school's associate professors at the time. The top employers were Arthur Andersen and Ford Motor Company (twenty each), Ernst & Ernst (twelve), and Coopers & Lybrand and Burroughs (seven each).

The 1976 undergraduate report indicated that the "typical 1976 BBA graduate was 22 years of age, a resident of Michigan, and a member of the brightest class ever to complete the rigorous BBA program. . . . Over 25% of the graduates were women, and approximately 5% of the class represented minority groups." The average starting salary was $12,600. The top employers were Peat, Marwick & Mitchell (six), Arthur Andersen and Ford Motor Company (four each), and Coopers & Lybrand (three).

According to 1974–75 Bulletins, typical costs for the MBA program, including tuition, housing, meals, books, and incidentals, were estimated at $2,975 for Michigan residents and $4,425 for nonresidents. The estimated undergraduate costs were $2,700 for Michigan residents and $4,200 for nonresidents.

Class sizes were small during the Wolaver era (Chapter 2), when the first graduating class totaled thirteen. One student recalled that, although he was the only student enrolled in a finance course, the professor encouraged him to take it, noting that "the School is new. We want a full curriculum. And you'd be the only student in class." The student remembered he "had to be prepared, because there was nobody else to call on."

By 1974, classes were much larger. My courses averaged forty-

3. The Business School at Age Fifty: 1974–75

eight students, and I called on them randomly (the so-called "cold call"). After class, there was often a long line of students in the hallway, waiting to see me during office hours.

Student activities in 1974 included participation on a student council and in a few student clubs: Beta Alpha Psi, the Marketing Club, the Management Club, the Finance Club, and a student chapter of the Society for the Advancement of Management. The student council also published a newspaper called the *Monroe Street Journal*.

In Loco Parentis. One of the significant changes from the 1920s to the 1970s was the relationship between the university and students, especially women students. Even as late as 1967, when I arrived on campus as a graduate student, the university viewed itself as a traditional parent in protecting women through housing, dress, and other restrictions. In a *Michigan Alum* article titled "Life Under Curfew" (Winter 2021–22), a 1968 graduate recalled, "It was to *protect* you, they would say. It wasn't the age of rebellion just yet. . . . We were used to men doing one thing and women doing another."

However, the late 1960s brought rapid change. The article noted these examples:

- Housing: "Women [previously] had to sign record books before leaving their residence hall or sorority at night, and they had to sign back in when they returned to show they made curfew. . . . By 1968, the U-M board of regents decided to remove the curfew for women for one trial semester if parents sent a permission slip requesting it, which 86% did. In 1970, they officially abolished mandatory curfews in residence halls."

- Dress: "Dress codes weren't dissolved on campus until the end of the 1960s. Before that, pantyhose were required for women attending Sunday sit-down dinners and jeans and

Bermuda shorts were allowed only on weekends."

- Michigan Union: "Women were not granted full and equal access to the Michigan Union until 1968. For many years, women were allowed in only through a side door and when escorted by a man."

- Michigan Band: "The U-M Marching Band was all-male until 1972, when several women auditioned and 10 made it. Before that, the head of the band, George Cavender, was quoted in the Daily as saying, 'It's more violent physical activity than would be proper for a lady.'"

Technology. Although the main form of technology in the 1974 classroom was the same as when the school was founded—blackboard and chalk—some professors used overhead projectors.

Outside of class, the school had a duplicating department. However, the use of the machines was restricted, and requests for copies required completion and submission of paperwork well before the copies were needed. I once taught at a Chinese university that was under surveillance because of its alleged participation in the Tiananmen Square protests. The way Communist Party officials guarded the copier at the university reminded me of photocopier restrictions at the business school in 1974.

The school maintained a laboratory where students could access electronic calculators and IBM keypunch machines. The university operated a computer center with a pair of IBM System/360 Model 67 computers that provided timesharing to the campus through fifty-five remote terminals, including four at the business school.

The most dramatic technological development at the time was offering TV courses. Classes were broadcast from a studio in Ann Arbor to classrooms in Dearborn and at Detroit area companies. My experience with TV teaching began in 1975. I could talk with the students at the remote sites, and they could see me on a screen in their classrooms.

Because I could not see the students, I placed their pictures under a camera when they had questions or comments. This arrangement created two concerns. First, I had to prepare to respond to the students' comments while searching for their pictures. Second, because I could not see them, I had no way of knowing whether they were watching Monday night football on a different TV screen when teaching on Mondays.

Teaching on TV was a wonderful developmental experience because it provided an opportunity for improvement through watching videotapes of the sessions. Among other lessons, I learned that I should never sit during class. TV courses also prepared faculty for future technology disruption that has transformed higher education, as noted in the next chapter.

Epilogue to the 1974–75 Academic Year

Developing lifelong friendships with former students is one of the great joys of teaching. One of my deepest friendships goes back to my first year at the business school when Makoto Toda enrolled in one of my courses. Nippon Life Insurance Company, currently the world's third-largest life insurance company, sent Makoto to Michigan for graduate study. We developed a close friendship that has lasted over fifty years.

In 2011, Makoto described this friendship in an article published in *INTOUCH*, a publication of the Tokyo American Club in Tokyo. Here is an excerpt from the article:

> Our friendship grew during my time in Ann Arbor. I eventually received my master's degree and returned to my job in Japan, often thinking about George and the generous help he had given me. My studies at the university served me well in my work, particularly after I was promoted to senior managing director and was placed in charge of the company's global headquarters.

I. Michigan Ross Then and Now

Like me, he enjoys drinking (whether it's beer, wine, cocktails or sake) and golf (although he's not entirely happy with his scores). And, like me, he thinks of himself as a tortoise, taking a steady and diligent approach to life and sparing no pains in his work.

George has continued to offer me advice over the years, encouraging me to carry on teaching at Aoyama Business School and Chuo University after I retired from Nippon Life. As our friendship strengthened, we formed the "Tortoise Club" in recognition of our similar attitudes, and our e-mails frequently contain tortoise jokes now. The membership of this exclusive club remains at two, but it inspires me to keep practicing my golf swing.

As a mark of respect for my lifelong teacher, friend and fellow tortoise, I composed a haiku: "One tortoise is crying, somewhere another hears."

The University of Michigan is fortunate to have accomplished alumni like Makoto who are willing to share advice based on their business success. For instance, my negotiation course includes cross-cultural negotiation. When I asked Makoto whether American negotiators should adopt a Japanese negotiating style when negotiating in Japan, his email reply noted the following:

> I definitely believe that Americans should stay with their own style. Of course it is important to respect the culture of each country. I believe if we respect each other, the negotiation will be a comfortable and constructive one.
>
> When I negotiated with the people from the USA, including Jim Robinson, former CEO of American Express, Richard Fuld, CEO of Lehman Brothers, or the people of Europe, including Dr. Breuer, CEO of Deutsche Bank, I felt very comfortable about their own style, although they were more straight-forward,

3. The Business School at Age Fifty: 1974–75

more open, more aggressive, and their attitude was more relaxed, especially the Americans. I think the success of negotiation between cross-national companies depends on respect of each other rather than style.

I have never seen better advice than Makoto's for cross-cultural negotiations.

Chapter 4

The Michigan Ross Centennial: The 2023–24 Academic Year

THE FIRST FIFTY YEARS of the business school's history, from 1924 to 1974, witnessed incremental changes, such as increases in degree programs (from one to four), faculty size (from fifteen to sixty-two), and student numbers (from twenty-two to 1,629). Classrooms and offices moved to a much larger building, student costs rose, and technology began to impact business education.

While similar incremental changes occurred during the next fifty years starting in 1974, by 2024, technology disruption had radically transformed management education. This chapter first describes the general teaching environment in 2023–24—the 100th academic year of the school's existence—and then discusses the changes from 1974 to 2024.

Teaching During the 2023–24 Academic Year

News at the start of the 2023–24 academic year included a war in Ukraine, an indictment of former president Donald Trump, the coronation of King Charles III, and the popularity of Taylor Swift and the film *Barbie*. The coronation brought to mind a week I spent in Washington, DC, in 2011 with BBA students admitted to the prestigious Carson Scholar Program at Michigan Ross. During one of our trips to the Hill, the students spotted Prince (later King)

4. The Michigan Ross Centennial: 2023–24

Charles walking down the steps of the Supreme Court. He stopped to talk with them, and the next day, their picture with the Prince appeared in a leading British newspaper.

Figure 4.1. Prince (later King) Charles with Carson Scholars

During the first week of class, an article in the *Michigan Daily*'s "Welcome to Michigan" issue noted that "coach Jim Harbaugh and his football team have their eyes laser-focused on returning to the College Football Playoffs." The team completed the season as national champions.

During the Fall Term, I taught two on-campus courses on "Negotiation and Dispute Resolution," one graduate and one undergraduate, with a combined enrollment of eighty-four students. I also taught an online course, "Successful Negotiation: Essential Strategies and Skills," offered by Michigan in partnership with Coursera. I

I. Michigan Ross Then and Now

continued to teach these courses after my official retirement in 2018, and 2023–24 marked my 50th year of teaching at Michigan Ross—one-half of the school's one-hundred-year history.

Route to School. I no longer walked to school as I did fifty years earlier, in 1974, but enjoyed the ride from my condo on the south side of Ann Arbor. I drove to the school around 7:00 a.m. to beat the traffic and occasionally meditated for a few moments at a spot with one of the best views of the campus—the elevated parking lot just north of the football stadium.

Sitting there on the first day of class (August 28) during Fall Term 2023–24, I opened the car window to enjoy the early fall temperature (low 70s on a sunny day). Behind the huge block M across the street on the stadium's north side sat a tall crane used to install massive new scoreboards, among the largest in the country.

Looking east, I saw Yost Ice Arena and the Intramural Sports Building (IM). The founding of the business school in 1924 was sandwiched between the opening of these two buildings—Yost in 1923 and the IM building in 1928. Several structures on the main campus stand out along the horizon left of the IM building, including Michigan Ross, the Ford School of Public Policy, the Law School, South Quadrangle, Burton Memorial Tower, and Munger Graduate Residences.

Class Preparation. The technology disruption discussed later in this chapter heavily influenced my preparation for class. Even without this disruption, my preparation differed from 1974 and reflected my fifty years of experience. An essential part of this experience resulted from the interaction with business leaders that characterizes Ross.

The "Negotiation and Dispute Resolution" course itself originated from a meeting I attended in New York City on November 30, 1983, with representatives of nine other leading business schools. We met at the invitation of Walter Wriston, the CEO of Citicorp. During the meeting, Wriston emphasized his concern about Cit-

4. The Michigan Ross Centennial: 2023–24

icorp's litigation challenges and encouraged us to offer courses on negotiation and alternative dispute resolution. At the meeting, I met the Stanford Business School associate dean, who later offered me a visiting professor position. I started teaching the negotiation and dispute resolution course after my return from Palo Alto to Ann Arbor.

My courses benefitted from contact with business executives when Executive Education was one of my responsibilities as associate dean. Teaching executives in Ann Arbor and worldwide enables faculty members to test degree program course content and develop new material that reflects current business concerns.

Former University of Michigan students were also helpful. For example, legendary investor Charlie Munger, who attended Michigan, sent me suggestions for teaching about decision tools and traps that arise during negotiations. Charlie passed away during the Fall Term, on November 28, 2023, at the age of ninety-nine.

Faculty colleagues. Faculty colleagues were another source of advice for course preparation and development. Occasionally, they would sit in on my classes (as I did in theirs) and suggest new approaches to teaching students how to make decisions at the intersection of law and business. As a result of a project funded by IBM, a colleague and I developed a case (and related software) on using decision trees to make litigation settlement decisions. Faculty colleagues at other schools where I had visiting appointments (Berkeley, Cambridge, Harvard, and Stanford) had also provided valuable suggestions over the years.

Feedback from students. Feedback from degree students is valuable in course preparation, as they often send me messages describing how they use course concepts and tools in their careers. Feedback from learners taking my online course, described later in this chapter, is also useful. As of this writing (in 2024), there are 19,502 course reviews online. They also send me emails, and on LinkedIn I have accepted thousands of invitations to connect with learners who share their stories about the impact of the course on their careers and personal lives.

Student names and backgrounds. Research on effective teaching emphasizes the importance of knowing student names. Using class cards with photos, I memorize them before the start of class so I can greet students by name when they enter the classroom for the first time. One challenge is that their pictures might be misleading and out-of-date. Someone with short hair, no facial hair, and no glasses might appear in class with long tresses, a beard, and glasses.

The class cards provide information about student backgrounds, which is useful when we discuss cases relating to their experiences. The cards also enable me to memorize the pronouns of students who have indicated preferences ("he-him," "she-her," "they-them").

Recent research and new concerns. Preparing for class requires reviewing recent research. In preparing for my Fall Term 2023 class, I reviewed thirty-four new articles I had collected over the six months since I last taught the course. I added them to course assignments, the PowerPoint deck, and teaching notes where appropriate.

Preparation for class in 2023 raised some relatively new concerns about trigger warnings and the cancel culture. When reviewing my course materials, I constantly asked myself whether the material might need revision because of its sensitive nature.

Students help me identify concerns. For example, a few years ago, I developed a cross-cultural negotiation exercise based on the real-life experience of a financial services company trying to sell its product on the Navajo reservation. I learned about Navajo values—which I deeply respect—during visits to the reservation. At one time, we sent students there to work on business development projects as part of our Domestic Corps program, which reported to me when I was associate dean. When a student expressed concern that some of her classmates did not respect Navajo values when doing the exercise, I enlisted her help revising the negotiation roles to eliminate the problem.

In the Classroom. I entered the classroom in August 2023 with more than usual enthusiasm following one year of teaching via Zoom during the pandemic and a second year when the students and I wore masks. Students in the class dressed in business casual (better than in 1974), while my faculty colleagues and I dressed more informally than fifty years ago—business casual instead of suit and tie.

The turning point in my dress habits occurred when teaching an executive course where the participants dressed casually. They jokingly demanded that I remove my coat and tie, which I did. They were amused when it came time for the course graduation a few weeks later, and I showed up without a coat and tie, not realizing that everyone was supposed to dress up for that occasion.

Over the fifty years following 1974, names used to address students and faculty had changed. I now addressed students by their first names, and most of them, at my invitation, called me George instead of Professor Siedel. I rarely cold-called students. I still used boards to capture key elements from class discussions and negotiation exercises, but the boards were now white instead of black and required markers instead of chalk.

Changes at Michigan Ross During Its Second Fifty Years

Michigan Ross experienced many changes during the fifty years that followed the 1974–75 academic year.

Degree Programs. In 1974, students could complete MBA coursework only through full-time and evening programs. By 2023, four MBA programs had been added: Weekend MBA, Online MBA, Executive MBA, and Global MBA. In addition, the school offered four one-year master's programs: Master of Accounting, Master of

Business Analytics, Master of Management, and Master of Supply Chain Management. Undergraduate students also had a new option: a fifteen-credit Business Minor program. As a result of this diversity of programs, working in the Registrar's Office has become one of the most challenging assignments in the school!

Multidisciplinary Action Projects. An especially significant change at Michigan Ross over the past fifty years was the development of action-based learning through the school's signature Multidisciplinary Action Projects (MAP) program. In a 2024 podcast, former dean Joe White described the origins of MAP. Before becoming dean, Joe left Ross for six years to serve as vice president for management development and public affairs at the multinational company Cummins. While there, he observed that "smart, well-educated people were a dime a dozen, but really effective people were much scarcer. . . . [T]he entire purpose [of MAP] was to enable our students to be better than students at other schools when it came to turning knowledge into action and action into results."

Through MAP, students can develop new businesses, advise existing organizations, manage investment funds, and lead ongoing business concerns. By 2024, over 17,000 students had participated in action-based learning in ninety-eight countries.

A 2024 *Poets&Quants* article described the difference between the students' experience and classroom learning:

> When it comes to learning new finance models, the basics of tried-and-true frameworks, or the complexities of business theories, the MBA classroom is great at laying the foundations. But when it comes time to put all those lessons to practice, there's no greater classroom than the real world. University of Michigan's Ross School of Business has been a leader in experiential learning for decades, creating unique in-the-field projects and courses for students to tackle real-life business challenges. It's also a leader in action-based sustainability, offering students the space

4. The Michigan Ross Centennial: 2023–24

and support to complete projects focused on sustainability challenges both big and small, at home and around the world.

Executive Education. By the 2023–24 academic year, Michigan Ross Executive Education had expanded to become one of the world's leading continuing education programs, having served over 20,000 participants and 3,000 companies. Named by the *Financial Times* as the leading provider in North America, the school also offered highly-ranked programs in South America, Europe, the Middle East, and Asia.

Participants attending in-person programs in Ann Arbor reside in boutique-style guest rooms at the Executive Learning and Conference Center on the Michigan Ross campus. Online and hybrid programs that blend in-person and online learning provide participants flexibility in scheduling. In addition to open enrollment programs that enable participants to interact with leaders from various companies, Michigan Ross is a leader in collaborating with companies to develop customized programs to meet their unique needs.

Although participants are not graded, they focus intensely on the learning experience while free from their usual work demands, often working late at night with their teams. Participants are not shy about sharing their experiences when they challenge ideas presented by professors and classmates. Working with business leaders enables faculty members to obtain feedback on their research and identify issues that are most important to executives, which they can use in further research and degree program teaching.

Faculty. Faculty size at Michigan Ross tripled between 1974–75 and 2023–24. The number of professorial (tenure-track) positions jumped in the 1980s when Dean Gil Whitaker decided that new positions were needed to reduce overload teaching so faculty could devote more time to research.

The number of clinical faculty and lecturers also grew substantially during the fifty-year timeframe. The faculty now includes several prominent members with appointments in other disciplines, such as music, psychology, and sociology. For example, when I retired, the Williamson Family Chair I held went to Scott Page, who holds appointments as a professor of political science, complex systems, and economics.

Faculty are organized into seven academic areas that match the key functions in organizations: accounting, business law, finance, management and organizations, marketing, strategy, and technology and operations. Another faculty area, business economics, is vital in laying a foundation for understanding the functional areas. And business communications faculty members provide students with the skills needed for communication in a world with multiple media opportunities.

Grading of Students and Faculty. As described in Chapter 3, there was evidence of grade inflation by the 1974–75 academic year. This was later held in check by the adoption of required grade distributions. For example, the MBA program uses five grades with the following distributions in required courses: Excellent (no more than 25 percent of students), Good (no more than 35 percent), Pass (no more than 35 percent), Low Pass or Fail (approximately 5 percent).

Student grading of professors through end-of-course evaluations has continued as in the past. Michigan Ross professors (who do not see the assessment before assigning grades) generally received high scores. Here are recent examples of the school's median evaluations on a five-point scale:

- [The professor] seemed well prepared for class meetings: 4.9

- [The professor] explained the material clearly: 4.7

Given these evaluations, it is no surprise that in 2023, *Princeton Review* ranked Michigan Ross as the leading school in its "Best Professors" category based on student surveys.

4. The Michigan Ross Centennial: 2023–24

Some faculty evaluations are available to the public. For instance, the website for my online negotiation course that Michigan offers on the Coursera platform contains (as of 2024) 19,502 reviews from learners in the course.

Faculty Research. Dedication to teaching does not detract from the school's research success, as Michigan Ross faculty members rank high in worldwide research rankings. They are supported by twenty centers, institutes, and initiatives focused on entrepreneurship, finance and accounting, international concerns, innovation and technology, leadership and organizations, operations, public policy and society, real estate, and sustainability.

The second fifty years of the school's existence witnessed an explosion of high-impact research by the faculty. This research has affected many aspects of the business environment. The president of the United States referred to faculty research on noncompetes in a State of the Union address. Faculty research led the president to issue an executive order on bank mergers. The US Supreme Court has cited faculty research extensively in a landmark decision on the liability of parent corporations for their subsidiaries' actions. Faculty research has influenced the development of legislation and regulations by administrative agencies in various areas, such as addressing corporate fraud in option awards.

Michigan Ross faculty research has had a significant impact on business practice in areas such as consumer behavior, emotional advertising, empowerment, fiduciary duties, franchising, global brands, growth strategies, production control methods, sensory marketing, social movements and organizations, sustainable enterprise, sustainable peace, and tax policy. Faculty members have originated concepts like core competency, factory physics, strategic intent, sense-making, and issue selling. They created movements like Bottom of the Pyramid and fields such as Positive Organizational Scholarship (which became a UM center) and Managerial and

Organizational Cognition.

Faculty members also created the Customer Satisfaction Index, which has played a vital role in developing firms' key performance indicators. They have led the creation of standards companies use when deciding whether to use corporate monitors in settlement agreements for misconduct. They have worked with major companies to create principles for corporate political responsibility. And courses taught by faculty have led to the creation of companies.

Facilities. In early 2003, I received a call from the Michigan Ross dean. He told me that one of our alumni, Steve Ross, was considering making a gift to the school and wanted to meet with some students. Six students and I had breakfast with Steve, and he seemed intrigued by the research projects they were completing. I hope this meeting contributed to his decision the following year to give $100 million to the school. In an article describing the gift (*Dividend*, Fall 2004), he commented on the strong work ethic of Michigan students, who are "just as bright as students" anywhere.

This naming gift enabled the school to replace "The Tower," which had housed the school since 1948, with a state-of-the-art facility completed in 2009. Four years later, Steve announced a second $100 million gift to fund spaces for collaborative learning and career services, classrooms with advanced technology, and student scholarships. At the same time, he gave another $100 million to the athletic campus for new facilities and programs to improve academic success. And four years later, in 2017, he announced a gift of $50 million to support career and faculty development and action-based learning.

4. The Michigan Ross Centennial: 2023–24

Figure 4.2. The Stephen M. Ross School of Business building at the University of Michigan

Thanks to the generosity of Steve and other Michigan Ross alumni, the school has a magnificent 5.6-acre campus that includes a large Winter Garden where students gather between classes, a Starbucks, an electronic trading floor, a café with food and drinks from the legendary Zingerman's Deli, and a fitness center. (The *Wall Street Journal*, April 22, 2017, featured the fitness center in an article on my tai chi exercise routine.)

Art and nature were important considerations when the school expanded. The facility provides students with a cultural experience through 250 works of contemporary art on display. In front of the school stands a magnificent oak tree that started life around the time America declared its independence from England. As part of the construction of the current facility, the 350-ton tree was moved around one hundred yards and transplanted in its current location at a cost of approximately $400,000.

Students. By Fall 2023, the number of students in Michigan Ross degree programs had grown to 1,984 graduate students and 2,333 undergraduates. The 379 students in the full-time MBA class of 2025 had an average GMAT of 719 and average work experience of 5.8 years. Forty-three percent was the magic number for the class—representing the percentage of women, the percentage of US students of color, and the percentage of international students (from thirty-nine countries).

The 818 students admitted to the BBA program in 2023 (out of 9,210 applicants) had an average 3.93 high school grade point average, an average SAT score of 1480, and an average ACT of 33. Forty-four percent of the class were women, and 6 percent were international. Fifty-five percent of the class were students of color.

Joint degrees, specializations, and minors. Attending a business school located in a world-class university provides students with opportunities to broaden their education beyond business. For instance, my Fall Term MBA course included students from the College of Engineering and students in a joint degree program offered by Michigan Ross and the School for Environment and Sustainability. MBA students in the course also pursued specializations in design thinking, healthcare management, and other areas.

One-third of the BBA students in my course minored in areas such as computer science, design, public health, entrepreneurship, public policy, history, real estate, and religion. Other BBAs in the course majored in subjects like communication and economics or were in joint degree programs.

Student clubs. Michigan Ross students participate in over 130 clubs and organizations. Some clubs focus on the key functional business areas, such as accounting, business law, finance, human resources, and marketing. Other clubs are reminders of the diversity that enhances the learning experience in and outside class. Examples include Asian, Black, Brazilian, Chinese, European, Hispanic,

Indian, Japanese, Korean, Latin American, and Taiwanese clubs.

Students with athletic and outdoor interests can join basketball, cycling, ice hockey, outdoor, pickleball, and soccer clubs. For refreshment following their activities, they can gather with members of the Maize & Brew Club or the Wolverine Wine Club.

Tuition. Tuition for students in the full-time MBA program for the 2023–24 academic year was $70,392 for Michigan residents and $75,392 for nonresidents. Other costs (including books and supplies, food and housing, and personal expenses) were estimated at $27,534.

Tuition for an entering BBA student during the 2023–24 academic year was $17,926 for a Michigan resident and $58,718 for a nonresident. Under the "Go Blue Guarantee," students from families in Michigan with incomes of $75,000 or less and assets under $75,000 received free tuition. Other costs (including books and supplies, housing and food, and personal expenses) were estimated at $18,324.

Career opportunities. Employment data for full-time MBA 2023 graduates indicated that the base median salaries across all industries were $175,000, with a median signing bonus of $30,000. Two-thirds of the employers were in the New York metropolitan area, on the West Coast, or in Chicago. Over 60 percent of the graduates went into consulting or technology jobs, and the top five companies were McKinsey, Bain, Boston Consulting Group, Deloitte, and Amazon.

The median base salary for 2023 BBA graduates was $100,000, with a median signing bonus of $10,000. Three-quarters of the employers were in the New York City area, on the West Coast, or in Chicago. Two-thirds of the graduates went into financial services or consulting, and the top five companies were PwC Strategy, EY Parthenon, McKinsey, Deloitte, and Bain.

I. MICHIGAN ROSS THEN AND NOW

In Loco Parentis. As noted in Chapter 2, when the business school was founded in the mid-1920s, the university acted *in loco parentis* in tightly regulating the students' physical welfare and accommodations in an authoritarian manner. Writing in *The Chronicle of Higher Education* (March 21, 2024), Rita Koganzon observed that "The old *in loco parentis* paradigm had . . . implied a familial relation, but a hierarchical one: Students were the children; faculty and administrators were the adults with punitive authority."

During the mid-1970s, colleges loosened the rules—especially for women students. And by the mid-2020s, Koganzon concluded, a "new paradigm emphasized the egalitarian, nurturing, and intimate elements of family relationships, while downplaying the hierarchical aspects. The new college experience was like home, but this time with cool, permissive parents instead of overbearing, restrictive ones."

At Michigan Ross, a strong emphasis on community values illustrates the "new paradigm" described by Koganzon. The school's Academic Honor Code provides examples of academic misconduct, and a Code of Student Conduct covers nonacademic misconduct such as misuse of community assets, disruptive conduct, and other forms of misconduct described in greater detail in the university's Statement of Student Rights and Responsibilities. The university statement includes examples relating to the safety of those who might be victimized by activities such as hazing, stalking, bullying, or domestic violence.

In addition to emphasizing community values, the university has become more supportive of students in ways that reflect modern parenting practices. At the beginning of each semester, my colleagues and I provide students with information about services available to advance their mental health and well-being. During the 2023–24 academic year, Michigan Ross appointed its first Director of Student Wellness, and the dean reached out to students with messages of support regarding COVID-19 and wars in Ukraine and the Middle East.

4. The Michigan Ross Centennial: 2023–24

These new forms of support create an opportunity for a more holistic relationship between faculty and students that extends beyond the classroom to meet student needs. For example, one undergraduate in my Fall Term 2023 courses suffered from the symptoms of long covid. Two students developed COVID-19 during the term, while others had COVID-19 symptoms but tested negative. A student missed class because of food poisoning. Others were absent following the deaths of close relatives, and one student faced distress after her dog was put down.

In these situations and others, I listened carefully to student concerns and helped them as best I could. As the chief university health officer noted in a Fall Term message to faculty, "often the most impactful interaction a student can have is receiving encouragement and guidance from you and their peers."

The Fall Term experience reminded me of teaching during the pandemic when I electronically entered students' living rooms, bedrooms, kitchens, and yards (on warm days) when teaching via Zoom. Witnessing distractions caused by family members, roommates, and pets provided a holistic perspective on their lives that was unavailable when they were students sitting in my class for a few hours each week. I saw them as complete human beings with problems and concerns similar to those we all face.

Rankings. In 1988, *Business Week* (now *Bloomberg Businessweek*) began publishing business school rankings regularly. *US News & World Report*, *The Financial Times*, *Princeton Review*, and LinkedIn, among others, followed suit. Business schools soon realized that rankings are important because they are used by applicants when selecting schools and by companies when deciding where to recruit.

Poets&Quants combines the five mentioned rankings, which it considers to be the most influential and credible. In its 100th year, Michigan Ross ranked 9th, according to this 2023–24 composite

I. Michigan Ross Then and Now

ranking. *US News* also ranks thirteen MBA specializations. According to *Poets&Quants* (April 26, 2023), "Only one school ranked in every one of US News' 13 specialization categories: Michigan Ross School of Business. It's a feat the Ross School has now accomplished for three straight years."

US News also ranks undergraduate business programs. In the 2024 rankings, Michigan Ross ranked No. 4 in the *US News* undergraduate specialty rankings, No. 1 in management and marketing, and in the top 5 in accounting, entrepreneurship, finance, and production and operations management.

Disruptive Technology. In a 2024 *Poets&Quants* article, Michigan Ross Dean Sharon Matusik noted that "I expect to see an acceleration in expectations for business schools to play an active role in addressing the grand challenges of our time." One of the challenges she mentioned was technology disruption. While "disruption" might have a negative connotation to some, the technology disruption at Michigan Ross has resulted in positive innovations designed to improve business education and practice. Here are personal examples of technology's impact on the school's teaching and research during the 2023–24 academic year.

Using Technology when Preparing for Class. I start my preparation by visiting a gateway to my course called Wolverine Access, where I place my textbook orders, find the location of my classrooms, and monitor the list of students. The student list provides photos, the students' majors, and preferred pronouns. A couple of weeks before the course begins, I use Wolverine Access to email the students, welcome them, and ask them to complete a pre-course assignment.

I use a link at Wolverine Access to visit Canvas, the course learning management system. I post the course syllabus, assignments, and readings here. My Canvas site also has links that enable students to find information about wellness programs and academic integrity standards.

4. The Michigan Ross Centennial: 2023–24

Course and research materials. When I started at the business school in 1974, my syllabi and negotiation exercises were handwritten and typed by my administrative assistants ("admins"). Although I prepare these Word documents myself today, the admins are very helpful in populating Canvas and handling other matters, such as providing cards with student pictures and background information. I use these cards to memorize student names and learn about their experiences that might relate to class topics.

In the past, I used copies of journal contents provided by the library to identify articles and books for use in my teaching and research. In an electronic age, the library, which contained 55,000 books in 1974, was reduced to twenty-two physical books fifty years later. I locate the latest research online, sometimes with the assistance of library staff.

IT support. To assist my class preparation, the Michigan Ross technology department advised me and other faculty members that the classroom PCs contained twenty-seven applications and asked if we wanted more. (I didn't.) They also sent a welcome message at the start of the new term, offering to meet in the classroom to review recently updated technology, such as screen-sharing technology for monitors at the perimeter of the classrooms and an enhanced confidence monitor. (I don't use a "confidence monitor" and had to google it to ensure I knew what the term meant.) The technology department followed its welcome message with seventy-two technology messages throughout the semester.

Videos and extended reality. I met with IT staff to review technology in the classroom and revisited the classroom later to test my PowerPoint deck. My main concern was whether the embedded videos would work and whether I could move quickly from the deck to various links. One of these links is a TED-Ed animation I created with Christine Ladwig that illustrates how to address an ethical dilemma when facing a product liability crisis. The video has generated over two million views at TED-Ed.

Another link is to an extended reality experience I created with a Michigan Center for Academic Innovation team in 2023. The 360-degree experience enables students to virtually enter an office where they make a pitch for an investment in their company, similar to the pitches made on the TV show *Shark Tank*.

Artificial intelligence. When preparing for class, I had to decide how to address AI concerns. The school prepared a Canvas site on GPT essentials that included thirty-two resources covering the basics of GPT models and how to use GPT in courses and research. For example, the site provided information about Maizey, an AI tool developed for Michigan faculty and students. Some of my Michigan Ross colleagues employed Maizey as a teaching assistant that handled around 350 questions per week for each class.

I used three approaches to address the use of AI in my course. First, I established guidelines on using and citing AI when completing course assignments. Second, in one of my research assignments, students compared the results of their research with the results produced by GenGPT. (They were surprised by the speed at which GenGPT produced its results but concerned about inaccuracies and what it missed.)

Third, I embedded coverage of AI into the course content. For example, when covering alternative dispute resolution, we explored using AI to prevent disputes, assess risks, and assist arbitrators. We also explored how AI might replace arbitrators and mediators in the future.

The Technology Experience in Class. Once class started, technology continued to influence my courses. During the first class, I reminded students that I would grade their class participation, and their grades would be lowered for inappropriate use of cell phones and laptops in class.

I used Wolverine Access to send emails reminding students of assignments due for the following class. I also emailed them the key learning points after each class. Students emailed me when they could not attend class because of illness, a death in the family, and so on. We then continued the email conversation to develop plans for them to cover the session they missed.

Virtual negotiation. I assigned an exercise where students negotiated with a classmate using their favorite platform (Zoom, Skype, WhatsApp, etc.). Following the exercise, they identified differences between virtual and in-person negotiations, indicated the one they preferred, and noted how they would prepare for future virtual negotiations.

Virtual office hours. Zoom was popular with students for office hours. In the past, office hours were scheduled at set times, sometimes resulting in a long line of students outside my office. With Zoom, I could easily meet with them anytime, day or evening.

In addition to talking about the course, students were interested in discussing uncertainty about their future. A 2024 report concluded that the United States, for the first time, was no longer one of the happiest countries in the world. Happiness had especially decreased among younger Americans. Experts cited in a *Wall Street Journal* article (March 19, 2024) mentioned causes (such as loneliness, fear about the future, world events, and money concerns) that undoubtedly contributed to my students' uncertainty.

Grading of assignments. During the course, students completed and posted five papers on Canvas, which required me to grade 420 papers in the two sections. Using Canvas helped me keep track of the papers and grade them efficiently. For example, after a long grading session, I occasionally become concerned that I have overlooked a student's discussion of certain concepts. The "Find" function (CTRL-F) lets me double-check my grading quickly.

Negotiation website. I created a website called "Negotiation Planner," which provides a course review with tools students can use during future negotiations. In addition to a general negotiation planning tool, the tools include an assessment of negotiating style, a guide to developing negotiating power, and a life goals analysis.

After Class Ends. In the past, at the end of a course, I posted student grades in a grade book, then totaled and submitted them on a prescribed form to the registrar. Today, an Excel grade sheet totals and sorts the grades, and I use Wolverine Access to submit them electronically.

Students also submit their anonymous grading of my performance electronically, using a five-point scale. After posting my grades, I receive the results of their ratings of the course (for example, "The course advanced my understanding of the subject matter") and me (for example, "[The professor] held students to a high standard"). I also receive their written comments on the strengths of the course and how it can be improved, which help me prepare for future classes.

Technology Costs. Preparing and using teaching-related technology requires significant time, which limits the time available to develop course content. Time costs were magnified when I taught my courses from home via Zoom during the pandemic. I had to learn how to share my screen, record sessions, set up breakout rooms, annotate materials, add captions, use the "raise hands" icon, and so on.

I also learned that, given technology glitches and a different style of interacting with students on Zoom, professors can only cover around 70 percent of the material taught in person. Among my other concerns were:

- the students' Zoom fatigue,

- the possibility of a power outage or hardware failure,

4. The Michigan Ross Centennial: 2023–24

- lighting adjustments,
- hacking by Zoombombers, and
- noise at home—such as the roar of my neighbor's lawnmower.

In retrospect, I was fortunate that there was only one technology failure where I briefly lost connection with students. Here are the reactions of two students who forgot the session was being recorded:

- Student A: "Did we lose him?"
- Student B: "Yeah. Awesome."

Communication with colleagues. In addition to humbling experiences like this and other Zoom challenges, another technology cost is more subtle. Email communication and text messages have minimized or replaced in-person interaction with colleagues. As an assistant professor during the pre-email era, I often visited the office of a senior colleague who offered valuable advice on teaching.

Later, as associate dean, my conversations with colleagues in the faculty lounge provided useful information about their concerns. For example, on August 19, 1996, faculty member LaRue Hosmer complained to me in the faculty lounge that faculty had no forum for sharing our current research, and he wished we could gather for monthly discussions over lunch. When I called his bluff by asking whether he would fund the lunches, he agreed to contribute $10,000 annually.

I immediately relayed Hosmer's offer to Dean Joe White, whose philosophy was that there should be a presumption of yes when new projects were proposed. Shortly after that, the school announced the creation of the Hosmer Interdisciplinary Research Lunch Series.

I. Michigan Ross Then and Now

Disruptive Technology Benefits. While technology costs are high, so are its benefits. In my degree courses, technology enables me to efficiently:

- order textbooks
- locate my classroom
- monitor class lists
- email students
- find, prepare, and post course materials
- grade papers that students have posted electronically
- prepare and use my PowerPoint deck
- tabulate and post grades
- develop videos (like TED-Ed), extended reality experiences, and AI assignments
- use communication tools like Zoom for office hours and incorporate the tools into class exercises
- prepare a website with tools students can use for future negotiations
- review evaluations that students submit electronically.

These technology benefits do more than support my course. They also launch students into a future where skills and flexibility are required to address continuing technology disruption.

MOOCs. Technology also enables me to offer courses to a worldwide audience of learners. Over 1.5 million learners have joined one of my massive open online courses (MOOCs) offered by

4. The Michigan Ross Centennial: 2023–24

Michigan on the Coursera platform. Class Central, a leading aggregator of MOOCs, has advised me that the course, "Successful Negotiation: Essential Strategies and Skills," is the most popular online business course in the world.

I receive messages constantly from learners from around the world, ranging from CEOs to novice negotiators, who have taken the course. They provide examples of how they use the course concepts and tools professionally and personally. Their stories validate the content of the course and provide suggestions for improvement that I incorporate into my degree courses on campus.

Research impact. Technology keeps me current with the latest research relating to my teaching and research and improves collaboration with coauthors. In the past, faculty research was disseminated mainly through peer-reviewed journals. Today, technology provides an opportunity for greater impact. For instance, our research dean collects and analyzes information regarding the number of our media cites, op-eds, and social media impressions.

Reverting to 1925—Going Tech Bare. While technology brings high costs—in terms of my time, staffing, hardware, and software—it also produces many teaching and research benefits. How does it impact the core learning activity: the interaction between teachers and students in class? This became more than a theoretical question when technology crashed at the University of Michigan at the beginning of the 2023 Fall Term.

Shortly before classes started on August 28, the university discovered that an unauthorized third party had gained access to personal information about certain students, alumni, employees, hospital patients, and others. In a message to the community early in the morning on the first day of class, Michigan Ross chief of staff Amy Byron-Oilar advised faculty and staff that the network was down, and there was no access to Google drives, Dropbox, Zoom, Wolverine Access, Canvas, and other systems.

As a result, when I walked into class later that morning, I was technology bare. In other words, in the 100th year of Michigan Ross, my classroom experience was similar to that of Doc Wolaver in 1925, as described in Chapter 2. The quality of the discussion that morning was never better. It was comforting to realize that, despite technology's influence on teaching and research, education is ultimately based on the human-to-human interaction between instructor and students that leads to a mutual learning experience.

PART II
LEGENDARY PROFESSORS

Chapter 5. William "Bill" Paton: Outstanding Educator of the Century

Chapter 6. Paul McCracken: A Modest and Influential Advisor to Eight Presidents

Chapter 7. Mary Bromage: Navigating the Shoals of Discrimination

Chapter 8. Al Edwards: A "Dean of Inspiration" Arrives After a Student Uprising

Chapter 9. CK Prahalad: The World's Most Influential Thinker

Chapter 5

William "Bill" Paton: Outstanding Educator of the Century

WHEN SERVING AS a visiting professor at Harvard Business School several years ago, I lived across the street from Mary Baker Eddy, who founded the Christian Science Church in 1879. She resided in beautiful Mt. Auburn Cemetery, which was dedicated in 1831 and was the first US cemetery where the graves were placed in a park-like setting. I heard a rumor that a telephone had been installed in Eddy's grave so that she could call for help if awakened from the dead. While living in the neighborhood, I did not receive a call and later learned that the rumor was false.

There are ties between Mt. Auburn and Ann Arbor. Photos of the cemetery are among the 250 works of art on display at Michigan Ross. Ann Arbor is home to Forest Hill Cemetery, a pre-Civil War cemetery modeled after Mt. Auburn. Set on sixty-five acres on the eastern edge of the Michigan campus, Forest Hill includes many paths named after the paths in Mt. Auburn.

Among the people buried at Forest Hill are the founders of Ann Arbor (John Allen and Elisha Rumsey), six University of Michigan presidents, and legendary football coaches Fielding Yost and Bo Schembechler. Yost's epitaph reads, "I wish to rest where the spirit of Michigan is warmest."

If you wander through Forest Hill past the many magnificent

monuments, you might miss a small marker on a grassy knoll on the eastern side of the cemetery. The headstone of one the most famous Michigan business school professors simply reads: "William A. Paton 1889–1991." At his request, there was no funeral service after his death.

Bill's headstone belies his impact on accounting and the business world. The title to his obituary in *The New York Times* referred to Bill as a "Pioneer Accountant, Theorist and Scholar." The national professional organization of Certified Public Accountants, AICPA, named him the Outstanding Educator of the Century.

Figure 5.1. Bill Paton

Bill Paton's Biography

Personal Background. Bill Paton was born in Michigan's Upper Peninsula on July 19, 1889, and passed away at 101 in Ann Arbor on April 26, 1991. His father was born in Scotland, and his mother's family in the United States dates back to pre-Revolutionary War times.

Bill grew up on a farm where life was rugged. As recounted by Kelly Williams and Howard Lawrence in *William A. Paton: A Study of His Accounting Thought* (2018), work on the farm began at 5 a.m. and concluded at 9 p.m. Bill later worked his way through college by washing dishes, waiting on tables, husking corn, and sawing wood.

The family was poor, and Bill remembered a diet "liberally loaded with dandelion greens, . . . cabbages, turnips, and other cheap vegetables." He didn't drink alcohol or smoke, and his frugal diet continued throughout his long life. He could have been the poster child for the benefits of a calorie-restricted diet when, at the age of one hundred, he prepared his own meals consisting of an egg for breakfast, no lunch, and cornflakes and raisins for dinner. His dinner menu undoubtedly would have the approval of a recent Kellogg's "cereal for dinner" campaign with the slogan "give chicken the night off."

Bill's healthy diet and habits of hard work on the farm contributed to his productivity. According to his former student Bill Pierpont, who served as vice president and chief financial officer at Michigan, "When he was writing a book, he'd work all day at the School of Business, then take two or three bananas and an apple, and head over to Rackham and write till two a.m. He'd spend several nights a week like that. He was a busy man. 'A lot to do,' he'd say, 'and only 24 hours in a day.'"

Bill married Mary Sleator, his sister's friend, and they had two sons and a daughter. In addition to their work on the farm, Bill's parents were educators, and Mary's family also had an interest in education. Her father taught physics, and her brother was a physics professor at the University of Michigan.

Bill's later interests included flying, track, and tennis. His son Andy Paton, also an accounting professor, shared his interest in tennis. A Big Ten champion at Michigan, Andy played in several US Opens and reached the second round when he played at Wimbledon. A tennis court adjoined the family home in Ann Arbor.

Education. Bill's association with the University of Michigan began when he was seven, and his father studied science at the university as a special student. Bill's educational accomplishments at Michigan are difficult to beat. Within three years, he earned an undergraduate degree (1915), a master's degree (1916), and a PhD (1917). He was the first to earn a PhD in accounting at the university.

Experience. Bill was a professor at the University of Michigan from 1917 until 1959, when he retired holding the titles of Professor of Economics and Edwin Francis Gay University Professor of Accounting. He also served as a visiting professor at several universities, including Berkeley and Chicago.

Bill was a consultant and expert witness in federal and state courts. Bentley Historical Library has copies of his testimony in sixty-one cases from 1925 to 1998. In Ann Arbor, he served three terms on the City Council and, as a CPA, founded an accounting firm.

Research. Bill published over twenty books on accounting and other topics, as well as over 200 articles.

Service. Bill was the founding editor of *The Accounting Review*. His government service included a position as Chief of Special Assignments at the Internal Revenue Service, then known as the Bureau of Internal Revenue.

Honors and Awards. Among Bill's honors and awards are the following:

- AICPA Outstanding Educator of the Century

- AICPA Gold Medal Award (first academic recipient)

- Accounting Hall of Fame (first academic member)

- Michigan's Paton Center for Research in Accounting (named in his honor)

- Fellow, American Academy of Arts and Sciences

- Honorary degrees from other universities

Superior Intellect

How did a poor farm boy become the outstanding accounting educator of the twentieth century? The characteristics that immediately come to mind are superior intellect, feisty personality, and compassionate teacher. Bill's intellect was neatly summed up by Joel Thompson in *History of Accounting: An International Encyclopedia* (May 1, 1991): "For Paton, using his mind was not just his profession, but his way of life."

Bill demonstrated his intellectual ability at a party at the home of friends Maynard and Mildred Phelps when playing a game to entertain a friend who was ill. This is Bill's description: "Maynard named 40 objects of thought, material, or otherwise, slowly, as I sat in a dark corner of the room with eyes closed. Mildred wrote the words down, in numbered sequence, as he announced them. He tried to embarrass me with ridiculous, lengthy 'objects' such as the 'average wage of a textile worker in a cotton mill in Bombay.' I then repeated the entire list of 40, in order, and for good measure also recited the list in sequence, beginning with the last 'object.'"

This intellectual ability, combined with his interest in students, enabled Bill to recall details about them years after they attended his classes. At a party when he turned one hundred, he reminded a

II. Legendary Professors

former student where he had sat in his classroom fifty years earlier.

In a speech at another event, a partner in a large accounting firm mentioned that Bill had given him a C in a course he had taken around forty-five years earlier. This is an account of what happened next: "At this point, Bill turned abruptly in his chair to look up at the speaker, waggled a finger under his nose, and declared, 'It was not a C, it was a C minus.' 'No Bill,' our speaker retorted, 'it was a C. I remember because it was the only C I ever received.' 'You're wrong, young man, it was a C minus. You failed to solve the consolidation question on the final correctly, and I was forced to lower your grade.' 'Well, I guess you must be right,' demurred the perplexed ex-student."

Bill's intellectual ability extended beyond numbers to a love of words. I experienced this firsthand when strolling down the hall with him one afternoon when he was in his mid-nineties. We walked behind a couple who appeared to be undergraduates. He was well over six feet tall, and she was a foot shorter. Bill turned to me with a twinkle in his eye and muttered, "Well, that's the long and short of it."

Bill's interest in words was evident early in his life when, as an undergraduate in 1913, he took a course called "The Short Story" offered by the Rhetoric Department. Students were required to write a short story, and during the last class, the professor read the best one. Although most students in the class were in graduate school, he chose Bill's story, "The Relinquishment." The story, which reflects his childhood interest in the macabre stories of Edgar Allan Poe, was published in *Dividend* (Fall 1976).

Bill's love of words continued throughout his life, and he once claimed, "I used to read 500 books a year." At the age of ninety-five, he published a book called *Words! Combining Fun and Learning*. In the book, he notes, "Words are man's greatest tool. Words are the basic building blocks of both language and thought." Citing a study published in the *Atlantic Monthly*, he concluded that a key to business success is the ability to use words.

5. William "Bill" Paton

The book is designed to strengthen the ability to use words by enabling readers to have fun with word puzzles and games. Here is an example of word play from the book published in *Dividend* (Summer 1984). To test your potential for business success, try to convert the letters in the first missing seven-letter word into three other seven-letter words in this rhyming puzzle. (*The answers are at the end of this chapter.)

> When Daddy-O in deep _____
> Puts baby Bill flat in a chair,
> And then in spite of yells and kicks
> Proceeds his _____ to fix.
> Smart wife complains, though very tired,
> "To that you should not have _____."
> But Grandma, coming in amazed,
> Declares that Daddy should be _____.

Feisty Personality

Dictionary definitions of feisty include lively, quarrelsome, spirited, determined, aggressive, courageous, spunky, forceful, animated, and tenacious. These all describe Bill. He was not shy when sharing his concerns about the country, the university, and accounting standards with presidents of the United States and the University of Michigan, cabinet members, and CEOs. There was no doubt about where Bill stood on the issues of the day. He followed the advice he gave to students: "Stay out of the middle of the road to avoid being run over."

Bill's feistiness and his penchant for hard work were apparent during his first job after he left the family farm in 1906. In an October 29, 1973, letter to Ford Motor Company CEO Henry Ford, he described his experience at one of the company's plants: "My daily wage was a fine $2. A brash country youngster, I supposed the way to get ahead was to pitch in hard, and in a few days, I had antagonized my fellow workers by my tactics. An older man one evening took me to one side and sternly warned me. 'Bub, if you don't stop showing off you're likely to have a monkey-wrench hit you on the head and it may not bounce.' Perhaps foolishly, I decided to quit. No doubt I should have been more adaptable and made my desire to do well less conspicuous."

Experiences like this, combined with his independent life growing up on the farm and the teaching of his mentor at the university, Fred Taylor, shaped Bill's views toward economics. He was a fierce foe of socialism and communism. As stated in his letter to Ford, "Ever since I began the serious study of economics in 1912, under a great teacher and logician, Fred M. Taylor, I have been doing my best to support the concept of an economy dominated by individual initiative, private enterprise, and a competitive market."

One former student remembers Bill as "red-headed, vigorous, willing to speak his mind and a rugged individualist." His feistiness was an important factor in his groundbreaking research. As a colleague put it, "He was not impressed with the sanctity conferred on an accounting method merely by long usage, he refused to kowtow to immediate expediency, he was a persistent foe of pussyfooting, and he was a poor compromiser."

In a letter to Bill on his 100th birthday, former colleague Bob Mautz noted, "You taught us to think for ourselves, to have courage to leave the beaten path, to nurture our own ideas, and to defend them with courage. You never felt constrained to follow the crowd if you thought the crowd was wrong."

Bill's obituary published in *Dividend* (Spring 1991) noted that "he moved the focus of accounting away from bookkeeping to a sophisticated process that went hand in hand with economic theory and modern corporate finance." Professor Norton Bedford concluded that Bill's research "did much to restore public confidence in the public accounting profession" after the 1929 stock market crash.

Bill could be feisty even when commenting on non-accounting

matters. One summer, a close friend of mine who was a junior professor at the time grew a beard. On spotting the beard, Bill told him he assumed it would be gone before classes began. It was! The same friend later negotiated the purchase of Bill's house. Bill abruptly ended the negotiations when my friend mentioned remodeling the kitchen. Bill advised him that the house was in perfect condition and needed no changes.

Bill's opinions on topics beyond accounting could be controversial. For example, during the McCarthyism era in the mid-1950s, the Economics Department wanted to give an unusual promotion (from lecturer to Full Professor with tenure) to a brilliant economist, Lawrence Klein. The Un-American Activities Committee of the House of Representatives learned that Klein had been a member of the Communist Party. When Klein admitted this was true and explained that he had left the Party, the committee did not require him to testify before Congress.

While sixteen members of the Economics Department supported Klein's promotion, Bill and another faculty member were opposed. When Bill bypassed the department and voiced his objections directly to the Board of Regents, which had to approve the promotion, Klein accepted a position at Oxford University. He later joined the faculty at Wharton, where he was awarded a Nobel Prize. In 1977, Klein received an honorary degree from Michigan.

Compassionate Teacher

During cross-examination in a case where Bill served as an expert witness, an attorney asked him, "What is teaching?" He replied, "[A]ll the work associated with the presenting of subject matter in classrooms and dealing with students as a result of that presentation which means preparation, consultation, setting of examinations, marking of examinations, conferring with colleagues about the program, committee meetings involving the question of the development of the curriculum and all that sort of thing—in fact the

II. LEGENDARY PROFESSORS

whole range of duties that fall to one as a teacher in an institution."

Herbert Taggart, Bill's long-time colleague, summarized the "dealing with students" part of his teaching: "No student who encountered him has forgotten his incisive mind, his impatience with sloppy reasoning, his endless stock of homely anecdotes and Biblical references, his interest in his students' careers, and his amazing ability to remember names and faces. He takes pride in never having sat down in the classroom and in a nearly perfect record of attendance at the appointed hours."

Former students appreciated Bill's dedication to teaching. According to Lynn Townsend, who served as CEO of Chrysler, "Without a doubt he was the finest accounting professor that our profession ever had." The former Minister of Finance and Deputy Prime Minister of Thailand, Amnuay Viravan, put it this way: "Professor Paton's teaching and fine example have led to the raising of accounting standards in the United States and many other places throughout the world. He is a light to us all."

Letters from Bill's former students sent to him when he turned one hundred provide strong evidence that he taught them far more than accounting. Through his compassion for students, he served as a role model for their lives after graduation. Here are examples:

- "If there is one set of characteristics that I admire most in Bill Paton, it is that he is a compassionate, fair person who cares about people." Harold Bierman

- "The thing that remains with me [after all these years] is your compassion for your students." W. L. Ammerman

- "On many occasions, I have publicly stated that you influenced my business career more than any one person. . . . The integrity you instilled in your students and the responsibility you displayed toward them distinguished you as a true 'professor.' The students in my era referred to you as a 'students'

5. William "Bill" Paton

professor'—someone who gave his students a higher priority than his other activities." L. A. Engelhardt

- "Some 35 years ago you imparted not only knowledge, but some important lessons in discipline and fairness to me and my fellow classmates." Tom Turner

- "I was down in the dumps comparing my achievements with some of my student colleagues. You understood my discouragement and gave me some advice that went something like this: 'Develop the practice of comparing your achievement at a particular point in time with what you personally were capable of doing. Don't whip your conscience with comparisons that leave you the short end of the stick.' My esteem and affection for you have made that advice especially meaningful throughout my life." Charles McKinney

- "[T]hank you for that special gift—for being a real life hero; someone to respect; someone to pattern one's own life after." Denny Arno

- "[Y]ou have motivated and touched the minds of many, many students in your classes, as well as scholars and others in your books, improving many minds along the way, with vast benefits to the communities where they live and serve." Kermit Moss

Paton's teaching contributed to the success of many business school graduates who achieved high-level leadership positions. Here are comments from former CEOs when Bill turned one hundred:

- "[A]s the years have passed, your high standards for logic, hard work, clear thinking, and doing the right thing are the impressions that stick.... Arnold Johnson, CEO, Magma Power Company

II. Legendary Professors

- "A large part of whatever success I have had I can trace directly back to you." Roger Smith, CEO, General Motors Corporation

- "You undoubtedly influenced my life through my business career more than any professor I ever had." William Jackson, CEO, Tupperware Worldwide

- "Your lectures for the first time stirred in me an appreciation of the creativity and sheer intellectual joy of business life." Everett Berg, CEO, EBCO Enterprises

- "[Y]ou had a greater impact on my professional life than any other single person. As a CPA, attorney and CEO of a then Fortune 500 company, I often was guided by your wisdom and philosophy." Russell Braga, CEO, SPS Technologies

Someone once asked Bill what he was most proud of. Despite his many honors, he responded, "Other than my family, it's my students."

In recent years, some commentators have questioned the value of a university education, suggesting that course content can be offered cheaply online by instructors who are not engaged in research. These commentators overlook the impact of professors like Bill Paton, who do far more than deliver dated content. Because they are active in research, Bill and similar colleagues understand and shape the latest developments in the field. Their skills enable them to select and bring to class the highest-quality research, which they use to help students understand where the field is headed. Professors like Bill are also able to share their own research and give students an understanding of the process used to create knowledge.

Unlike those taking courses offering canned content, students who study with professors like Bill leave university with an understanding of the fluid nature of knowledge and an ability to contribute to its development. Their learning process is accelerated by what has been called the "peer effect," the stimulation provided by participating in live classes with other students who are talented, enthusiastic, and willing to challenge conventional thinking.

In an era of easy access to content through AI, learning from professors like Bill to ask the right questions and to identify reliable information for decision making is more important than ever for future success. In the words of historian Henry Adams, who was quoted in a *Dividend* article on Bill, "A teacher affects eternity; he can never tell where his influence stops."

(*The answers to the word play: despair, diapers, aspired, praised)

Chapter 6

Paul McCracken: A Modest and Influential Advisor to Eight Presidents

WHEN HE WAS in his nineties, Paul McCracken often ate lunch near Starbucks in the Michigan Ross Winter Garden. Dressed in a suit and tie, he usually ate a hamburger after removing the top half of the bun—although, at 5'4" and an estimated 140 pounds, he certainly had no concerns about being overweight.

Small in stature, Paul was a giant in developing US public policy. Michigan Ross professor Marina Whitman noted in her memoir *The Martian's Daughter* (2012), "A wisp of a man who looked as if he would blow away in a high wind, McCracken had the courage of a lion." Students walking through the Winter Garden on the way to class had no idea they were passing one of the most influential economists of the twentieth century.

Faculty members relished the opportunity to sit with Paul and listen to his stories about US presidents and business leaders. For instance, I enjoyed hearing about his first trip to Japan, where he met with Eiji Toyoda, the head of Toyota Motor Company, at a time when the company was trying to penetrate the US market. Mr. Toyoda expressed concern to Paul that the company would not be successful because its cars were not powerful enough to drive up high hills in the US. Later, Toyota obviously resolved this concern.

6. Paul McCracken

Figure 6.1. Paul McCracken

Paul McCracken's Biography

Personal Background. Paul was born on December 29, 1915, and passed away on August 3, 2012. His obituary in *The New York Times* was titled "Paul W. McCracken, Adviser to Presidents, Dies at 96."

Paul grew up in a Quaker family of farmers in Iowa. Years later, he betrayed his farming roots when growing rhubarb for his wife's pies at his home in Ann Arbor.

II. Legendary Professors

In an *Ann Arbor Scene Magazine* article, Paul recalled, with his characteristic humor, several life lessons that began at his one-room elementary school. Paul's foremost honor at the school was winning a contest for "the most impressive facial contortions in the gum-chewing match. Thus early in life I was to learn the important lesson that no one in this world is left wholly devoid of aptitude for something useful."

Paul's gum-chewing talent did not prove useful in high school:

In September, 1929, I confronted the spine-chilling challenge of entering Richland High School—a formidably large educational institution with an enrollment that year of 87. This experience was not without its challenges. For example, each morning and evening there was a trip in a 1929 Model T, which, hopefully, could be cranked into reluctant activity if a rear wheel were first elevated with a jack. In high school there proved to be no scope for my gum-chewing talent, and I thus learned early another important lesson—city people (Richlanders in this case) cannot automatically be counted on to appreciate the finer things of life.

Moving on from gum chewing, Paul noted that he turned his "extra-curricular efforts to such lesser things as forensic work, in which I did reasonably well until the Methodist minister's son came along. (In retaliation I finally became a Presbyterian.) Thanks to the fact that two bright co-eds in our high school class moved away before the senior year, I found myself, to practically everyone's surprise, the valedictorian in 1933. Thus, I learned a third important lesson in life—if you want to succeed, the task is made much easier if the competition will withdraw."

While in high school, Paul was asked to play right tackle on the football team, making him one of the most undersized linemen in the sport's history. According to his close friend and confidant Herb Hildebrandt, an emeritus professor at Michigan Ross, he "played for about 10 minutes before twisting his knee, and his budding sports

6. Paul McCracken

career came to an end."

On entering William Penn College in Oskaloosa, Iowa, in 1933, Paul observed that he turned his "attention to pacifying the College farm hogs with the kitchen garbage. (That is to say, I was told that this was my 'self-help' job.) I persevered, working my way up the garbage supply line, until in the second semester of my senior year, I was the second man in the pot-and-pan-washing department in the College kitchen. And thus was enabled to learn life's fourth important lesson. Garbage does not become significantly more attractive the closer one gets to its origin."

After graduating from William Penn, Paul met his wife Ruth when teaching at Berea College in Kentucky. The couple had two daughters.

Education. Paul received his BA degree from William Penn College in 1937. His MA (1942) and PhD (1948) degrees were from Harvard University.

Professional Experience. Paul taught English at Berea College from 1937–40. He later recounted that when he graduated from William Penn, the Depression-era "labor market was able to control its excitement about my entry, and there proved to be no great clamor for my services." So, he eagerly accepted an offer to teach English at Berea. "I knew very little about teaching English, but that was a detail when the salary was announced to be $1,500 per year."

Paul's room and board expenses were only $23 a month, so he saved enough to attend Harvard during the summers. After leaving Harvard, Paul worked from 1942–48 at the US Department of Commerce and as research director at the Federal Reserve Bank of Minneapolis.

Paul joined the business school in 1948 as an associate professor and retired as a chaired professor in 1986. In a letter dated June 23, 1948, Dean Russell Stevenson informed him of the appointment and that he had found a two-bedroom apartment for Paul. His starting salary was $6,000.

A letter dated July 27, 1948, from faculty colleague Ollie Blackett advised Paul that his textbook order had been placed at bookstores. Blackett suggested a Tuesday-Thursday-Saturday teaching schedule. Teaching on Saturdays, he noted, would give Paul more time to meet with business leaders during the week. In his previous job at the bank, Paul had a private office with a secretary. At Michigan, no offices were available, so he worked from a desk in Blackett's office.

Over the years, Paul took leaves of absence from the university to serve on the US President's Council of Economic Advisers, chairing the CEA during the Nixon administration. He was also on the *Wall Street Journal* Board of Contributors and wrote over eighty articles for the *Journal*.

A Year in Paul's Life. Paul's annual report to the dean in 1974 (the year I arrived at the business school) provides a snapshot of the breadth of his activities:

- Courses taught: 4

- School committee assignments: 2

- Service on commissions, boards, and councils: 8 (For example, he was president of the Conference Board on US-Japan Economic Policy.)

- Publications: 4 articles, 1 book chapter, 10 *Wall Street Journal* editorials

- Talks: 28 (to an estimated total audience totaling over 6,400) plus testimony before Congress (twice)

- Corporate Directorships: 7 (These directorships included S.S. Kresge Co., Lincoln National Corp., Detroit Edison Co., and

6. Paul McCracken

Hoover Ball & Bearing Co. Not listed in his report were other companies where Paul held director positions during his career, such as The Dow Chemical Company, Sara Lee, Johnson Controls, and Texas Instruments.)

- Other: Two weeks in Europe on behalf of the US State Department and two weeks in Japan for the Asia and Yoshida Foundations

Honors and Awards. Paul's honors and awards include:

- University of Michigan Distinguished Faculty Award (1959)
- Appointment as the Edmund Ezra Day Distinguished University Professor of Business Administration (1966). (As described in Chapter 1, Day was the business school's founding dean.)
- Paul McCracken Master of Business Leadership Program at William Penn University named after him
- Recipient of eight honorary degrees

Paul McCracken's Communication Skills

The three sections following this one focus on Paul's public service, teaching, and personal traits. A thread linking these aspects of his life was his ability to communicate in a common-sense manner. Paul honed his communication skills at William Penn College: "I probably had the best course in freshman English that one could possibly have.... [The professor] was a stern woman, large—she probably was close to six foot tall—and no nonsense. Not mean, but just no nonsense. As I told my daughter once, we learned English because we didn't dare not learn."

Paul further developed his communication skills when teaching English at Berea College. He mentioned this experience when praising Joe White for his performance as business school dean in a letter dated March 17, 2000:

> This is just a quick personal note extending to you my gratitude for the magnificently effective leadership you have given our Business School during these years. . . . [The school] is solidly established in the top echelon of Schools of Business Administration—and in a "market" that is international and intellectually exciting in ways undreamed of during my early years. For that we shall forever be indebted to you. Another quick note. (As you may know, my earliest years in pedagogy were spent teaching English at the preparatory school of Berea College.) Your letter was a magnificent piece—one which could well go into an English composition book on the way it ought to be done.

Paul refined his writing skills while writing his doctoral thesis at Harvard. As he noted in an interview, "I believe that Francis Bacon says, 'Writing maketh an exact mind.' I learned there [at Harvard] that the statement, 'Well, I know what I want to say but I can't seem to say it,' is a contradiction in terms. If you can't say it, you don't know what you want to say."

Early in his career in public service, Paul was encouraged to write concisely when he met with President Eisenhower about his appointment to the Council of Economic Advisers. As Paul remembered Eisenhower's comments, "The main thing, he said, is always to give us the straight dope; let's never start out by kidding ourselves. He paused a moment, flashed the famous smile, and added that he never wanted a memorandum more than one page long, but he wasn't sure that was possible for an economist."

Other presidents appreciated his communication skills. According to President Nixon, in a tribute on Paul's 75th birthday, "He was an intellectual. He knew all the big words, but he used words average people could understand."

An essential aspect of communication is engaging in dialogue

6. Paul McCracken

and listening respectfully to the other side. Paul stated his philosophy on listening to the other side's point of view in a blunt letter to an assistant minister who used the pulpit one Sunday morning to criticize US military spending. During church services at the First Presbyterian Church in Ann Arbor, I would occasionally daydream during sermons by wondering whether Paul (whom I could see as he sat with his wife Ruth near the middle of the nave below the balcony where I dreamt) was concentrating on the sermon or thinking about a current public policy concern.

I learned from the following December 11, 1978, letter to the minister that Paul indeed paid close attention to sermons:

> This letter is not written in the spirit of anger but because I believe you would do well to ponder further the sermon which you preached last Sunday. . . .
>
> A major underpinning of your remarks is the assumption that *we* are keeping the arms race going—that if *we* would only signify our good intentions by disarming we could have a peaceful world and remain secure. *They* are simply responding to our bellicose ways. . . . During the last decade the "real" volume of our resources devoted to defense has, in fact, declined 35 percent. . . . If your hypothesis is correct, we should be receiving more amiable vibrations from the U.S.S.R. than seems to be occurring.
>
> Let me be quite blunt. Frankly, I have never been much impressed that the geo-political wisdom of theologians is any better than that of other laymen, and nothing that I heard Sunday caused me to alter this evaluation.
>
> My most serious concern, however, is with the implied moral arrogance of those who hold your position. I can and do honor and respect many whose views differ from mine. There is no

scope for dialogue, however, if one insists that those "on the other side" are motivated by venality while our motives are pure. . . . I have known a good many corporate executives, Admirals, Generals, Secretaries of State and Defense, and even a few Presidents, and I do not find them any less dedicated to keeping this nation free and at peace than you and your colleagues (or any less intelligent). There is one difference. They do have to face, and face squarely, the question: If we do this, what is a reasonable expectation about the results? Not only the immediate consequences, but the secondary and tertiary consequences. And they cannot evade responsibility for those consequences.

This letter is written in no spirit of pique or vexation. Nor, however, are these spur-of-the-moment ideas just to let off steam. Let me at least urge you to state your case in such a way that there can be a dialogue between people each of whom begins his statements with an implied: "I may be wrong, but . . ." I did not detect that in your remarks yesterday. And a fruitful dialogue will never occur if one side or the other insists that it has moral superiority.

Paul's interest in dialogue based on respect for the other side probably contributed to his appointments as an advisor by both Republican and Democratic presidents, as discussed in the next section. President Richard Nixon noted in a letter dated April 3, 1986, "Your leadership of the Council of Economic Advisors was outstanding in every way. But what particularly impressed me was that while you never hesitated to express your honest opinions you were always willing to listen to the views of others who disagreed with you and were big enough on occasion to indulge in a little self-deprecating humor." If only today's politicians shared Paul's ability to listen to the other side.

Paul McCracken as an Influential Advisor to Presidents

Paul is especially well known for his service as an economist who was influential in the development of public policy. In the words of Nobel Laureate Paul Samuelson, he was the "archetype of 'an economist's economist.' Presidents and Senators have known him as a companion in arms for the task of developing sensible modern wisdoms."

The University of Michigan Regents echoed Samuelson's sentiments when they named Paul professor emeritus upon his retirement. They described him as a "distinguished teacher, eminent scholar and economist of international acclaim."

Paul was incredibly influential because he had the ear of arguably the most powerful person in the world, the president of the United States. His influence was not limited to presidents. Boxes at the Bentley Historical Library are filled with letters to and from members of Congress, ambassadors, cabinet members, Federal Reserve officials, and business leaders that evidence his behind-the-scenes influence on topics such as the impact of a bill on inflation, sugar prices, oil imports, energy policy, and bank reserve requirements.

Most of these letters are on a first-name basis, and nicknames are common. A letter to Senator Jacob Javits begins, "Dear Jack." Secretary of Commerce Maurice Stans becomes "Maury." Paul addressed Secretary of Defense Caspar Weinberger as "Cap." And so on.

Paul was also on a first-name basis with many presidents, with whom he was friends. In commenting on President Gerald Ford, Paul noted that "we were personal friends, close friends for a long period of time, our paths crossing in more casual environments than in formal meetings."

But no matter how close he was to presidents before their election, Paul's presidential letters always began with "Dear Mr. President." He followed the same convention in his correspondence with foreign dignitaries: "Dear Prime Minister" (to British PM James Callaghan), "Dear Mr. Chancellor" (to German Chancellor Helmut Schmidt), and "Dear Mr. President" (to French President Valery Giscard d'Estaing).

Here is a summary of Paul's role in advising presidents whose terms in office spanned 1945–1993:

- Harry S. Truman: Senior Economic Advisor

- Dwight D. Eisenhower: Council of Economic Advisors

- John F. Kennedy: Task Force on the Domestic Economic Situation

- Lyndon B. Johnson: Commission on Budget Concepts

- Richard Nixon: Chair, Council of Economic Advisors

- Gerald Ford: Special Consultant on Economic Policy Proposals

- Ronald Reagan: Economic Policy Advisory Board

- George H. W. Bush: National Steering Committee

In addition to these formal advisory roles, presidents sought Paul's advice on an informal basis. Here are some comments from Paul and the presidents illustrating his formal and informal advice.

President Eisenhower. Paul recalled, "I wouldn't want to suggest that Ike and I became buddies. So my book, Me and Ike, wouldn't be very long. I guess I would see Eisenhower as a complex person who could be anything from the Eisenhower of the $1 million toothpaste smile to the mule-skinning Army general."

Paul's last meeting with Eisenhower, at Walter Reed Hospital

6. Paul McCracken

where Eisenhower was a patient, was a sobering lesson on the fleeting nature of life. As Paul put it, "A President may be the most powerful person in the land, yet is underneath as human as the rest of us, especially when lying in a hospital bed."

According to Paul, they talked privately for over an hour. "[T]hree months later I was in Washington's big cathedral attending his funeral, which, of course, was an eerie experience, to see Charles de Gaulle, and the King of Belgium and the Prime Minister of Great Britain, and people like that being escorted down the aisle."

President Eisenhower expressed his appreciation for Paul's advice in a letter dated February 3, 1959: "Your services since 1956 as a Member of the Council have been immensely valuable. . . . I am sure that there will be times when we shall need to call on you for further consultation on economic questions and I trust that we may do so as the occasion demands."

President Kennedy. Paul recounted that after a report was presented to Kennedy, the president "winked, turned on the smile that was destined to charm and captivate the world, and said, you know, you don't write like a Republican."

Working with presidents like Kennedy, Paul quickly learned the realities of political life. For example, Kennedy commented on a recommendation in the report that made sense, but "here's the problem. That legislation would have to come out of the Senate Finance Committee, and Harry Byrd would go . . . right through the Capitol dome if I proposed that. So I don't think I can."

According to Paul, "We did our job as advisers. We alerted him to a problem. I'm sure he made the right decision, that the political cost of doing that was not worth it, that he would have to give up too much on more important things. I've always remembered that."

President Nixon. According to Paul's obituary in *The Washington Post* (August 5, 2012), when President Nixon asked him to chair the Council of Economic Advisers, Paul told him he first wanted to

II. LEGENDARY PROFESSORS

discuss it with his wife. "Nixon and I talked a while longer and he said, 'You know, I have a press conference coming up in about 20 minutes, and I don't have anything to tell them. Why don't we just announce it?' . . . So I said, 'Well, okay. I guess my wife can find out about it on the news.'"

Nixon later wrote, "During the most difficult hours of my first term . . . I came to depend on Paul both for his incisive intellect and his hard-headed pragmatism. He was a key adviser during a crucial time in our nation's history."

In a June 22, 1972 letter, Nixon thanked Paul for "providing me with your insights and suggestions on means of improving our relationship with Japan. Your thoughts were most timely. Henry Kissinger pursued in general a number of your ideas with the Japanese and found them quite receptive to working out means of improving our relationship."

President Ford. In letters sent in October 1974, the president thanked Paul "for taking temporary leave from your academic duties at the University of Michigan to come to my assistance in Washington" and expressed his gratitude for "your counsel during the economic summit conferences. Having the benefit of your knowledge and expertise in economics was of tremendous assistance to me." In a June 11, 1991, letter, Ford stated, "My economic policy views, while in Congress, in the White House and today are proudly based on the McCracken philosophy. I was honored to be one of your students, and thank you for your many kindnesses."

President Reagan. In a letter dated March 13, 1981, President-Elect Reagan thanked Paul for serving as Chairman of the Inflation Policy Task Force: "The considerable time and conscientious labor involved in developing policy recommendations, proposing appropriate personnel, and accommodating the range of people interested in working with us could not have succeeded without your assistance." Later, as a member of Reagan's Economic Advisory Board, Paul had monthly meetings with the president at the White House, except when Reagan was recovering from the assassination attempt by John Hinckley.

President Bush. Paul's advice was valued even when he had no formal role in a presidential administration. Future President Bush invited him to meet at Kennebunkport on August 18–19, 1978, to discuss whether he should run for president.

Bush's secretary followed this invitation with a note containing the schedule and logistical details: "You will need to bring a bathing suit, rain gear (just in case), and a sweater for the evenings. . . . Mrs. Bush will supply the bug spray—and one and all are invited to join her on the beach each morning for jogging!!"

The meeting was followed on February 18, 1979, with an invitation typed (poorly) by Bush to serve on his national Steering Committee. After he left the White House, the president wrote to Paul, "I often think back to the days when you and I were both laboring away in Washington, D.C. I continue to have only the greatest admiration and respect for you."

Other presidential candidates sought Paul's advice. On April 26, 1974, Senator Charles Percy invited Paul to a "completely private" dinner at his home in Georgetown. He described the purpose of the meeting:

> As you may know, I am presently exploring the possibility of running for President in 1976. While there is still time to think and plan before the usual chaos of a potential campaign, I am anxious to sit down and talk with you and a few others I admire who have given serious thought to this country—where it has been, where it's going, where it *ought* to go, what is possible and what is not. If I am to give a sense of direction to America, increasingly I need and want to be exposed first-hand to the ideas of those who have a longer perspective than someone so caught up in the day-to-day minutiae of government. Unfortu-

nately, the long view is a rare commodity among elected public officials in Washington.

Paul McCracken's Teaching

Sidney L. Jones, a prominent economist who worked closely with Paul and published the leading biography on the impact of his work (*Public and Private Economic Adviser*), commented on Paul's appointment to the University of Michigan faculty: "This world-class university provided an optimum environment for family and professional development and he has served it with remarkable devotion and distinction.... McCracken quickly established a positive reputation as a conscientious and skilled teacher with unusual interest in the development of students willing to meet his rigorous standards for class preparation and participation."

Given his work in Washington at the center of political power, Paul was especially well-positioned to combine theory and practice in the classroom. In his words, "There is merit in being able to bring to a class true-to-life stories on the complicated process of running a government, especially its economic policy. To cast a stone is easy, but when one is involved in the process it is easy to discern that application of economic theory is a highly complex matter, rarely deeply understood by the casual newspaper writer. Giving to classes the pragmatic and political nuances, both playing out simultaneously, was for me both invigorating and stimulating."

Paul's ability to respect the other side's views contributed to his effectiveness as a teacher. According to an article in the *Dividend* (September 1986), "When challenged in class, he would listen and discuss both pluses and minuses of an issue. He was sensitive to being dogmatic and concerned that students not be forced to accept his view but be left to form their own." His former student Martha Seger, who served on the Board of Governors of the Federal Reserve System, noted that Paul was "a very caring teacher interested in students as people."

Students benefitted from Paul's inside knowledge of government and the business world. A letter from President Reagan on Paul's retirement noted that "The people you have trained and guided at The University of Michigan ... constitute a force representing yet another of your significant contributions to our country's well-being."

Faculty colleagues also benefited from Paul's contacts in the political and business realms. For instance, Paul shared a memo he received as a member of the Dow Chemical Company board of directors in which the Dow CEO emphasized the importance of legal issues in new product innovation and development. I used this memo in class when discussing the legal framework for business decision making.

Paul McCracken's Personal Traits

On Paul's retirement, the University of Michigan Board of Regents observed, "Above and beyond all his accomplishments, it can truly be said that Paul McCracken is a humble man and a humane and considerate gentleman." These traits are readily apparent in hundreds of letters Paul wrote thanking or congratulating friends, colleagues, and even strangers.

At a time when he was a world-famous economist with many demands on his time, Paul wrote each letter by hand. His secretary then typed them with the onion-skin copies that now reside in over fifty boxes at the Bentley Historical Library. As the following sample indicates, Paul personalized each letter.

- To someone in the Development Office: "That was both awesome and disappointing news about your moving on to have larger and University-wide responsibilities for Development. They surely picked the right person, but we shall miss you here."

II. Legendary Professors

- To a colleague: "Your ability to discuss international financial and economic developments in a way that makes the subject fascinating is fast becoming legendary and Monday night was another illustration."

- To a secretary upon retirement from the business school: "Yours has been a model of effectiveness and good humor, a combination all too rare. I remember, of course, your arrival from the Upper Peninsula, and things then just started to function better."

- To a retiring Athletic Director: "This is a tardy letter, delayed by some travel extending as far north as the Yukon, to extend to you my deep appreciation for what you did during your tour of duty as Athletic Director."

- To his car dealer: "This is just a note to compliment you on your Honda service organization. I have found them effective in dealing with problems and thoroughly pleasant in their inter-personal relationships. Give them a pat on the back."

- To his heating contractor: "This is just a quick note to thank you for your coming to our rescue last weekend incident to the water heater problem."

- To his travel agent: "Your people have continued the Conlin tradition of unfailing courtesy and indefatigability in their efforts to assist with my sometimes vexatious travel requirements. With this letter I do extend to you once again, and through you to all your colleagues in the organization, my gratitude."

- To a retiring librarian: "The purpose of this letter is somewhat more formally to express to you my own deep sense of gratitude for your leadership in the School's library activities over the years. . . . Your performance here has certainly been brilliant, for which we are all in your debt."

- To emeritus professor Margaret Tracy: "Not too long ago, while I was talking to him about something else, the President [Ford] inquired about [you]. According to him, he was in one or two of your classes, and he remembered you with great fondness."

- To a research associate at the Law School on a recent publication: "That last monograph deserves more than simply an oral comment. It is a superbly written piece, and frankly I benefitted a great deal from it."

- To the business school dean (Joe White): "At the year end when congratulations and honors are being passed around it is easy to remember the professors and equally easy to omit another deserving member of the academic family—namely, the Dean. I do want you to know that I think you have been doing a remarkably good job in a responsibility that is not very easy."

Who takes time to thank auto dealers, heating contractors, and deans? Paul McCracken! Paul even sent congratulations to strangers, some of whom later became friends. For example, in 1981, Paul wrote to "Dear Professor Duderstadt" to congratulate him on his appointment as dean of the College of Engineering.

By 1990, after James Duderstadt became Michigan's president, a more personal letter to "Dear Jim" recommended Dean Gil Whitaker for the position of provost. "He knows the University thoroughly, and I believe he understands what is going to be needed if the University implements a strategy of assuring that the suit being cut from the available cloth will be an excellent one. He is easily underrated on the basis of casual conversation, but by now his track record

II. LEGENDARY PROFESSORS

here of demonstrated performance is surely an excellent one." Gil received the appointment as provost.

Another former Michigan College of Engineering dean, Charles Vest, recalled a note he received from Paul following his appointment as president of MIT: "Among the many notes of congratulations I have received on this appointment, one really sticks out in my mind. It was a brief note I had from Paul McCracken, one of the most distinguished members of our faculty. That letter said, almost in its entirety, 'Boy from West Virginia becomes president of MIT: The American Dream.'"

Paul's letters provided one of the most important lessons I learned when writing this book: the importance of expressing gratitude. The irony is that at a time when communication has never been easier through email and text messages, expressing gratitude has become a lost art.

What is the source of Paul's humility and gratitude that persisted despite his powerful role in government? A clue can be found in his diary. On March 14, 1939, when Paul was twenty-three, the following entry in his diary expressed his youthful frustration at trying to find purpose in life: "Tonight I would gladly have exchanged the latter half of my life if someone could have pointed me to an absolute that could command an unfailing devotion and allegiance."

In an entry eleven days later, on March 25, 1939, Paul identified one absolute that seems to have influenced his life: "'All men are created free and equal' . . . is the ideal toward which we strive and with which we start." Throughout his life, he considered everyone—from the president and other world leaders to people at all levels in the local community—as equals, treating them with compassion, dignity, and respect.

Chapter 7

Mary Bromage: Navigating the Shoals of Discrimination

THE ADMISSION OF women to the University of Michigan had a rocky start. As noted in *The Making of the University of Michigan: 1817–1967*, when the Michigan legislature recommended admission in 1867, "The Regents and President Haven recoiled like true men and said no." According to Haven, "Youth is a transitional period when passion is strong and restraint is feeble, and if, just at this period, multitudes of both sexes are massed together not in families and not restrained by the discipline of the home circle, consequences anomalous and not to be cultivated by an Institution supported by the State are likely to ensue."

By 1870, the Regents had a change of heart. They allowed Madelon Stockwell, the first woman student, to enroll in the university.

Early Years at the Business School

In 1924, the year the business school was founded, the Michigan Alumni Association surveyed the 10,258 women who followed Ms. Stockwell as University of Michigan students. A publication describing the results, *Women's Voices: Early Years at the University of Michigan* (2000), concluded:

> Experience of the early women at the University was as diverse

as the women themselves. While some reported fair treatment, others found injustices. Faculty were perceived as having differing degrees of acceptance; most were perceived as fair; some faculty treated female students with respect, even kindness. But some members of the faculty were critical and regarded women with contempt. . . . Competition with male students was perceived in various ways, as stimulating, and yet often as unfair. A lasting resentment was felt by many alumnae for the lack of support and encouragement from the University in obtaining positions. They sensed that encouragement and support were given generously to male students. They bitterly resented the University's failure to place women on the faculty.

As noted in Chapter 2, the business school's first graduating class in 1926 included one woman, Sih Eu-yang Chen, from China. She was one of nineteen women (out of 336 students) who earned MBAs during the next ten years. Comments from these early MBA students, as reported in the *Dividend* (Fall 2006), were mixed. According to Ailene Bardsley, MBA '33, women were "very welcome. Everyone was scared of Paton but he was a wonderful professor and very tolerant of us gals, there were so few of us."

But Helen Sandford, MBA '28, experienced discrimination that "began with the University of Michigan itself. When I was about to graduate with the MBA degree, I was advised to return to teaching, even though my adviser said that as far as IQ was concerned, I was second in the class."

Professor Margaret Elliott Tracy

Hiring Margaret Elliott Tracy as the first female faculty member was a bright spot in the business school's early years. She was born in Lowell, Massachusetts and completed her undergraduate degree at Wellesley College. She then worked in the personnel field for the government and in the private sector, where she was Personnel

7. Mary Bromage

Director for Waitt and Bond, Inc.

After completing her graduate work at Radcliffe in 1924, Professor Tracy joined the business school faculty, where she taught Personnel Management and was promoted to full professor in 1931. Following her retirement in 1950, the Board of Regents paid tribute to her contributions "as a brilliant scholar, a stimulating teacher, and a wise counselor of students." One of her students, President Gerald Ford, often expressed appreciation for her teaching.

Figure 7.1. Margaret Tracy

Professor Tracy published a book and articles on the earnings of women in business and the professions. Her 1928 article in *The Michigan Alumnus* (coauthored with Grace Manson) was titled "College Education for Women, Does it Pay?"

II. Legendary Professors

Based on data from 14,073 members of the National Federation of Business and Professional Women's Clubs, the answer was that "women who graduate from college earn more than women in lower educational groups." However, Professor Tracy also wondered why seventy percent of the women who graduated from college were employed by educational, social, or welfare organizations instead of commercial work. The article concluded that "The question of causative factors deserves consideration."

One "causative factor" was the possibility of discrimination. For example, during the Depression, it was felt that women should not take jobs away from men, who were responsible for supporting their families. During the height of the Depression in 1933, the business school sent a recruiting letter to businesses, suggesting that they consider hiring male graduates.

The letter stated: "If you could use a wide-awake young man in your organization this spring, we would like to have an opportunity of recommending to you a member of the graduating class. We realize that in the present conditions your recruiting program will be very greatly curtailed, but we do find from time to time that organizations are making places for young men who they want to get started before business picks up to such a point that there will be an active demand for the best men available."

Progress in 1970

Discrimination continued long after the Depression and was addressed in a lead article titled "WOMAN'S PLACE?" in *Dividend* (Fall 1970), one hundred years after women were first admitted to the University of Michigan. The article cited a study indicating that 84 percent of women and 77 percent of men "agreed that women are denied equal opportunity in business." For instance, government figures in 1968 showed that women with four years of college earned barely more than men with eighth-grade educations, and they earned only 58 percent of male college graduates' salaries.

7. Mary Bromage

The article summarized results from a survey of Michigan BBA and MBA female graduates. As in the 1924 Alumni Association study, the results were mixed: "Some are torn between career and family, some are full of zest for achievement, some are discouraged, and some are bitter."

The University of Michigan was not immune from discriminatory conduct. Publication of the *Dividend* article coincided with a letter from the US Department of Health, Education, and Welfare (HEW) to President Robben Fleming on October 6, 1970. The letter included several allegations of discrimination, including the following:

- Interviews "revealed that females are being discouraged from continuing for PhD training by departmental counseling."

- "Discriminatory hiring practices have resulted in underutilization of women in faculty positions at the University of Michigan."

- "It was reported during interviews that some women faculty members were being paid less than men of the same rank and background."

- "There are jobs at the University of Michigan that are segregated by sex, and the 'female jobs' are the lower paying secretarial and clerical jobs with little status, responsibility, or opportunity for advancement."

As discussed in the next chapter, Fleming had negotiated with members of the Black Action Movement a few months earlier. However, he attempted to distinguish issues relating to equal treatment for women from racial problems: "There are extraordinarily difficult problems in establishing criteria for what constitutes equal treatment, and we believe they are quite different from the now familiar problems in the field of race." Despite Fleming's concerns, Michigan completed negotiations with HEW by December, resulting

II. LEGENDARY PROFESSORS

in a *Michigan Daily* headline, "HEW Accepts U Proposals to End Sex Bias in Employment."

The effort to end discrimination in businesses and universities continues today. Women also bear a disproportionate burden in balancing work and family, an issue noted in the 1970 *Dividend* article: "Over and over, those who answered our questionnaire recognized the difference between the career-oriented and the family-oriented woman. . . . The woman most painfully caught in the family-career crunch is neither single minded about a career, nor content to stay home with the children and do volunteer work."

How did female faculty members navigate the shoals of discrimination and work-life balance during the pivotal years of change in the middle of the twentieth century? The career of Professor Mary Bromage provides a case study.

Figure 7.2. Mary Bromage

Mary Bromage's Biography

Personal Background

- Born October 13, 1906, in Fall River, Massachusetts
- Passed away on January 3, 1995, in Berkeley, California
- Husband Arthur Bromage (Professor of Political Science at Michigan) and daughter Susanna Bromage Paterson

Education

- Radcliffe College, BA 1928 *summa cum laude*
- University of Michigan, MA 1932

Publications. Over one hundred publications. Her books include:

- *Writing for Business*
- *Cases in Communication*
- *Writing Audit Reports*
- *DeValera and the March of a Nation*
- *Churchill and Ireland*

Professional Experience

- Reporter for two Boston newspapers
- Teacher at Buckingham Private School
- Teaching Fellow, Department of English, University of Michigan
- Lexicographer, Early Modern English Dictionary

II. Legendary Professors

- Assistant to Director of Civil Affairs Training Program, US Army
- Deputy Director of Training, UN Relief and Rehabilitation Administration
- Acting Dean of Women, University of Michigan
- Chief Editorial Writer, *The Ann Arbor News*
- Professor, Ross School of Business, University of Michigan
- Seminars on writing around the world for companies, the State Department and other governmental agencies, and the armed forces

Honors and Awards

- Freedom Foundation Award for "bringing about a better understanding of the American way of life"
- Hall of Fame, US Department of Commerce, and awards for teaching excellence from other government agencies and branches of the armed forces, including the Department of Agriculture, US Army, and the National Guard
- Citation of Honor, University of Michigan Board of Regents (a rare award to "individuals who have made extraordinary contributions to the life and welfare of the university." The award stated: "Your dedication to clarity, cogency and honesty in writing has earned an international reputation. . . . And you possess that rare attribute which marks every great teacher: an open and questing mind.")
- Mary C. Bromage Collegiate Professorship of Business Administration (honoring Mary's career)

7. Mary Bromage

- Arthur W. and Mary C. Bromage Fund (honoring Mary and her husband by providing student scholarships)

Mary Bromage's Career

Mary Bromage's international renown as a teacher and researcher occurred after she cobbled together various positions earlier in her career. The following elements of her life and career were gleaned from an interview, a speech she gave at Radcliffe on her 50th reunion, an article in *Glory: A Magazine for Interesting Women*, and an unpublished memoir called *Fall River and Beyond*. These resources are located at the Bentley Historical Library.

Early Interest in English Literature. Mary's deep love of English literature was ignited in high school when she discovered a copy of *Pride and Prejudice* in the local library. Later in life, she mentioned that teaching English literature "would have been a great joy, but circumstances did not permit it at that time." She also loved creating literature, as evidenced by her short stories and plays at the Bentley Historical Library.

Radcliffe College. At Radcliffe College, where she was an undergraduate, Mary's class voted to give pewter bowls to the first six graduates who got married. She said that was the college's goal—"not the first six women who got a job or went back to graduate school." Mary won one of the bowls when she married Arthur Bromage.

When Mary graduated from Radcliffe, the dean asked her what she was going to do. Mary said, "Well, I guess I am going to teach school." The dean replied, "Well, now, Mary, let me tell you something. You should not wait too long to have a family."

Early Experience with Discrimination. Mary faced discrimination when, as a student, "discrimination was so inbred, we (women) had to be grateful for small favors. This made our progress much slower."

After Mary moved to Ann Arbor in 1929, she was hired as an assistant to two professors in the English Department. The first professor readily agreed to her appointment.

Mary's conversation with the second professor was abbreviated. This is her account: "'Professor, my name is Mary Bromage and I've been appointed to be your new assistant.' Whereupon he flung down his pen, pulled his own chair back from the desk and looked me over from head to toe and said, 'No woman will ever assist me.' I think it was all I could do to walk out of the office."

Mary later attempted to pursue her dream of teaching English literature by applying to the PhD program in the English Department at Michigan. She recalled:

> I had always thought I could do whatever I liked, whether I was a girl or not. But these faculty to whom I applied for admission to the PhD program said, "Why should you want a PhD?"
>
> And I said, "Because I might sometime want to teach here." And they said, "No woman will ever teach in our English department." And I said, "Why not?" Well, they didn't seem to think they had to give me a serious explanation because I remember Professor Campbell, who always was a joker and who really had been very nice to me, said, "In self-defense."
>
> Well, as it was to prove over the years, too late for me unfortunately, our English Department did employ women. They had to do it. But I should never have allowed myself to be discouraged. I gave up too easily.

Acting Dean of Women. Mary served as Acting Dean of Women at Michigan from 1944–1950. The Dean of Women, Alice Lloyd, was diagnosed with cancer shortly after Mary was hired. As Mary recounted, "It meant everything in the world to her to continue as Dean of Women, even after she became too sick after a number of operations for cancer to come near the office. So for a while I did her job and mine. I would go at the end of every day to her house.... And as long as she was wide enough awake and well enough, she wanted to hear all the details of what had happened. So until the day of her death, March 1, 1950, she remained Dean of Women."

Some of Mary's duties were mundane, such as addressing a bread crust controversy in boarding houses for women (called League Houses). As Mary noted in a letter dated February 17, 1947, "I am writing in regard to the mistake about the serving of toast in League Houses. At no time has our office authorized any decision by League House mothers whereby girls who do not eat crusts should not be served toast."

Other aspects of the job were more serious. "What it really meant was that you had to be a friend and counselor ... to the women students. And you had to see that they were properly housed. And if they had problems with family affairs or love affairs, or they didn't like their courses, or they had to be asked to leave the university because they were failing, and any other kind of problem, you had to deal with those matters."

As Acting Dean of Women, Mary proposed policy changes that were radical for the times—sometimes with surprising reactions. For example, when she proposed allowing women to remain out of their dorms until midnight, "The men students didn't want that, because ... they would have to keep the girls out, the girls would want to stay out, and the men students, some of them, just didn't want to stay out."

Chief Editorial Writer for *The Ann Arbor News*. Mary covered many topics as Chief Editorial Writer for *The Ann Arbor News* from 1950–55. Here is a sampling:

- *On the need for university leaders to recognize the demands made upon women*: "Women not only vote, not only own the major share of the money in this country, not only enter into community affairs, but also contribute materially to the support of dependents in their families." July 9, 1954

- *On Ann Arbor bicyclists*: "Bicyclists obey no law of state or nation, no law of reason, above all, not the laws of the Ann Arbor traffic ordinance, which applies to them just as much as to automobile drivers." October 5, 1953 (Her comments resonate with Ann Arbor drivers today.)

- *On panty raids*: "Where there were at one moment hundreds of orderly, sober-faced youths, there are the next instant thousands of yelling, racing, wild-eyed infidels who follow some leader who does not really know what or where he is leading. . . . Next come the girls' part in the performance. Hanging out of their windows with come-hither cheers, they aid and abet their fellow students." May 21, 1953

- *On racism*: Officials in Sioux City, Iowa refused to allow burial in a local cemetery of a Native American soldier who died fighting in Korea. "By law, or better still by living deed, the United States must wipe the practice of racism from every town, every city and even, it seems, from every cemetery in the country." September 6, 1951

The newspaper rarely rejected Mary's editorials, although she recalled one time "that was amusing. There was a proposal by the city council to reduce the speed limit to 25 miles between a certain point and Pittsfield village, and I wrote an editorial supporting it. The editor . . . said that he couldn't print that. I asked why not. He said, 'I drive that every night to see my girlfriend and I don't want to cut it down to 25 miles.'"

Experience as a Professor. Mary felt that her appointment at the business school was fortunate because her husband was at another college within the university, and "there was a theory of nepotism, that I couldn't have taught in the same college where my husband was teaching. I later looked that rule up. I wanted to find it, and there is no written rule."

Mary's experience at the business school was generally positive: "I really loved it there." Although at one time, she was the only female faculty member, her male colleagues supported her, and she appreciated the "friendliness in the School."

Mary did observe discrimination against female students. "[There were] very few women students. Such women students as there were formed a women's club here, of which I was their sponsor. The women students at the time were not allowed to join the honor society that was recognized for professional purposes." As a result, women were denied a form of professional prestige available to men.

Mary also recalled:

> There was one very large course that was being given where, when a woman would put up her hand to recite, the professor would say "Sir?" And that went on, and there were other questionable jokes apparently told. . . . The women students went in to the dean, and I think the professor mended his ways.

> [W]hen it was proposed in a faculty meeting that women students be accepted for something . . . one faculty member, a senior person, said, "Well, of course, if we are going to admit more women, we'll have to change our requirements. . . . We'll have to drop the requirement for mathematical accounting courses." . . . He soon heard other views expressed from the floor by other faculty members who were as shocked as I.

Views on Careers and Marriage. Mary felt that "Marriage and a job are not inconsistent. If her partner accepts her career role, she makes a better working person. . . . There were great difficulties. I would be very tired when I would get home. I needed the help of my husband and daughter. But marriage should be the helping of each other to grow."

Mary acknowledged the love and support of her husband Arthur in a diary entry on September 10, 1979, when she traveled abroad (to Seoul, Korea) for the first time following his death. "I've been thinking of that one person, lost to me in the presence forever, . . . but forever with me in memory (as long as *I* live). His kindness, grasp, unspoken magnitude of understanding are a loss to me."

Career Advice. "[M]y own conclusion is that if you keep at wanting to work long enough and hard enough, and you're flexible and you're humble enough to take whatever job you think you can do and work hard at it, eventually you make that job into something that can give you real satisfaction."

Observations on Writing

Earlier chapters on Professors Paton and McCracken have noted the importance of communication in career success. As Professor Paton put it, "Words are man's greatest tool. Words are the basic building blocks of both language and thought." Citing a study published in the *Atlantic Monthly*, he concluded that a key to business success is the ability to use words.

What perspectives can an award-winning communications professor offer to those who aspire to leadership positions? Mary's timeless advice in a 1974 *Dividend* article ("The Game of Authors") still rings true in an age of email, text, and social media communications:

- The language [of good writing] has its own principles of clarity and brevity: concrete words, . . . short definite statements, . . . low-hurdle paragraphs to break down the insurmountable wall of words which long paragraphs erect.

- It takes a logical and disciplined mind to produce a logical and disciplined communication.

- Indecision makes its presence known in ambiguity and circularity of sense.

- Above all, knowing the readers and their hopes and fears is an obligation incumbent upon the managerial communicator.

- The crowning value of practical writing is its pinpointing for the sake of the reader. Audience-orientation is indispensable. . . .

- [Executives practice] two professions: the science of management and the art of written communication. . . . Their writing goals are to inform and convince.

What Makes a Good Teacher?

An article in *Dividend* (Spring 1975) posed the question "What Makes a Good Teacher" to university president Robben Fleming and selected business school faculty members and students. Mary's contribution exemplifies the characteristics that led to her success in the classroom:

- Excitement about one's subject.

- A belief in the moral values at stake.

- A curiosity about and concern for youth.

- Ability to change and recognition of change.

- *Not knowing all* the answers, but seeking more.

- Humor, tolerance, compassion.

Shortly after she retired, I asked Mary what she would miss most about teaching. She became teary-eyed when replying, "I will miss working with the young ones."

II. Legendary Professors

Epilogue

The 1970 *Dividend* article (reporting a survey of female business school graduates) concluded, "Many felt strongly that each woman who proves her ability makes it a little easier for the next." Mary's career was followed by a surge in hiring women faculty members at the business school. Some of these faculty members had already achieved prominence before joining the school. For example, Marina Whitman was a senior executive at General Motors, and Madeleine Albright served as Secretary of State before joining the Davidson Institute at the business school.

Others have held high-level positions at the University of Michigan. For instance, Janet Weiss, the Mary C. Bromage Collegiate Professor Emerita of Business, served as the Vice Provost for Academic Affairs and Dean of the Rackham Graduate School. Women have held many leadership positions at Michigan Ross, including three of the last four deans: Dean Alison Davis-Blake, Interim Dean Francine Lafontaine, and current Dean Sharon Matusik.

Women have also created leading programs at the business school. For instance, Sue Ashford joined the school after becoming the first woman to be tenured at Dartmouth's Tuck School of Business. An award-winning scholar, she served as the Michigan Ross senior associate dean and was the driving force behind the creation of the Executive MBA program, which she led for many years.

On July 1, 1970, three months before President Fleming received the HEW letter alleging discrimination (described earlier), visiting professor Mary Maples Dunn wrote him, describing her experience at Michigan. She was on leave from Bryn Mawr College and later became president of Smith College. In her words:

> In the first weeks of the summer term, many girls came to talk to me. Most of them volunteered the information that I was the first woman professor they had met and studied with, and they were intensely curious about me. They wanted to know how and why

7. Mary Bromage

I had decided on such a career, whether I am married and have children, whether I neglect my children, how I cope with these multiple roles. It was a novel experience, and I concluded that at Michigan the students have far too few models to suggest to them the wide range of intellectual and professional choices they can make.

As mentioned in Chapter 4, women comprised almost half of the BBA and full-time MBA classes admitted in 2023. Thanks to the path cleared by pioneers like Margaret Tracy and Mary Bromage and the leadership and achievements of female faculty members who followed, these students have access to excellent role models as they plan their lives and careers. Hopefully, their plans will include paying it forward to future generations of students.

Chapter 8

Al Edwards: A "Dean of Inspiration" Arrives After a Student Uprising

DURING THE MICHIGAN ROSS centennial year in 2024, the University of Michigan reexamined its free speech policies. A protest during the annual Honors Convocation triggered this review. In a message to the university community on March 26, 2024, President Santa Ono noted, "Like many of you, I am proud of our university's history of protest. But none of us should be proud of what happened on Sunday. We all must understand that, while protest is valued and protected, disruptions are not. One group's right to protest does not supersede the right of others to participate in a joyous event."

The president's reference to the "university's history of protest" brings to mind events that transpired over fifty years earlier, when business school dean Floyd Bond had to exercise unusual leadership skills to prevent bloodshed at the school. Reflecting on his eighteen years as dean, Bond concluded that these events were "the most traumatic, because we didn't even know if our house would be there when we came home."

The Black Action Movement Strike

Dean Bond was referring to the Black Action Movement (BAM) strike during the Winter Term of 1970. BAM was a coalition of student organizations that wanted to increase the enrollment of African American students. Dean Bond agreed with this goal and was frustrated when his attempts to increase enrollment were unsuccessful. He became especially concerned when a 1965 study revealed that half of the top nineteen business schools had no African American students, and the other half averaged one student per school.

The 1965 study triggered a series of actions designed to increase the number of African American students at the business school beyond its one student in 1966. Dean Bond summarized these actions in a report to the Regents dated May 17, 1973:

- A special faculty committee developed several recommendations, including partnering with the Tuskegee Institute to understand why the school was not able to attract African American students.

- In 1966–67, nine faculty members visited Tuskegee, where they taught a business administration seminar to encourage students to apply to the business school. Representatives were also sent to other universities with large African American enrollments for the same purpose.

- In 1967–68, Michigan African American students were included in recruiting visits to colleges with large African American enrollments.

- In 1968–69, a business school faculty member spent an entire semester teaching at Tuskegee. (During this time, Dean Bond personally developed close ties to Tuskegee, and after his retirement, he donated his professional library to the university.)

- Paul McCracken also held seminars at several colleges on behalf of the United Negro College Foundation to encourage enrollment.

II. LEGENDARY PROFESSORS

Dean Bond was disappointed with the results. By the Winter Term of 1970, the school had enrolled only sixteen African American students, three of whom were in the full-time MBA program.

Bond was also frustrated by what happened in March 1970, during the height of the BAM strike designed to close down the university. Dean Bond's following recollections (drawn from the Stephen M. Ross School of Business Oral History Interviews at the Bentley Historical Library) are slightly edited and organized by questions I added.

Why was the business school targeted during the BAM strike? "[T]he BAM movement became a fairly violent movement in trying to close down the University. We asked ourselves why we had been hit, because we weren't having any problems with our students, and the best answer that any of us could give was that we represented the establishment."

Did faculty and students think that the school should join the rest of the campus in closing down? "[T]he question of whether we should close down bothered, I think, the faculty, and the students, too, in our School probably more than most. For example, the tactics used to close us down were to disrupt the classes, and so a group of students would come in with tin pans that they had obtained in one of the dormitories or some of the kitchens around campus, and they would have a paddle, and they would bang on these tin pans in the classroom."

Were outsiders involved in using these tactics? "[W]e know that there were several outside students on our campus, and they were provoking this violence, which was the thing that was so bad about it. In fact, they were the ones, I think, that were really trying to get an incident where there would be bloodshed and this would give them publicity. . . . What they were looking for was publicity in the national press, and we were trying to avoid that, of course."

Could you provide an example of how the strikers disrupted classes? "We had a very, very popular professor teaching Business Law by the name of Professor Dykstra. [H]e was conducting a lecture . . . and the disrupters came in with pans and walked down the corridors banging so that you couldn't hear anything. He was of Dutch ancestry, and he was not one to give up. So he descended from the platform in the front of the room . . . and he faced the students and, in effect, by talking to them he actually pushed them back through the corridor and outside the door, and closed the door and locked it.

"So they poured through [another door] and came in. There were so many of them that he thought it was hopeless, so he went to the board. . . . And he started writing his lecture on this. And he proceeded to write the lecture, and the students were copying it. The noise was unbelievable.

"He ended up saying, 'It's three o'clock. End of lecture.' And he came right to my office, and he was shaking. . . . Students later confirmed everything. They said it was miraculous what he did. Education was important to him, it should go on. . . . [I]t was about three months later that he had a heart attack and died. I will always think that this was one of the reasons."

What else happened? "We would have fires started in our wastebaskets. Faculty began to go into their classrooms and lock the door. I will always remember, for a couple of days, the Associate Dean did nothing but roam the halls, and I began to do nothing but roam the halls, just to keep peace. They weren't our students, and yet, what do you do? The word we had received from the administration was to save the building if we could, but we could not call the police. No dean was to call the police."

How did the business students react? "I felt sorry for the students who wanted an education and were not part of this BAM strike. They really wanted to have the classes meet. They wanted the program to go on. They didn't want the end of the semester. . . . So there was pressure from those people, on the Student Council, and from the Student Council on us, to keep the School open. So we were trying to keep it open."

Did you ever feel personally endangered? "One day I came into the lobby and I heard this tremendous racket on the second floor above me, and I wondered what in the world was going on. So I went up. There was a whole group of about 40 students, none of whom I recognized. They were very young. I think they were undergraduates, if they were enrolled at all. It was about half black and half white.

"Outside this particular professor's room, there happened to be a fire hose and they had undone this and were getting prepared to take the hinges off the door and open the door and open the fire hose and give everybody a good bath with water. Now, these were the kind of disruptive things that they were doing.

"I'll always remember this, because there were three rather big guys getting that fire hose ready. I had never seen these fellows on campus. I didn't know who they were. But I walked through to them. Most of the rest of them were just sitting on the floor around, watching these three people. And I walked right through them.

"It was kind of a courageous thing to do, but it was probably a crazy thing to do as well. But I felt so strongly about what was going on that I walked through up to them, and I looked at one, and I looked at the second one right straight in the eye, and I looked at the third one. And I said, 'You know, if I were you, I wouldn't do this.' And I looked at each one of them again, and turned around and started to walk away.

"Boy, I got out of there fast. And I didn't hear any noise. I listened to see if they were going on. Pretty soon, I started back to the office. First, I waited where they couldn't see me to see if they went on with this because if they did, I was going up again. But they left

8. Al Edwards

that hose exactly where it was, and the hinge on that door was half off, and they left and went out."

Do you recall any other examples? "[An informant who didn't identify himself called and said] 'There is a gang on their way to put your library out of commission. They'll be entering your building in four to five minutes. I don't know what to do, but I want you to know.' [A faculty member, Walt Kell, and I] went up there and immediately I called the librarian over and asked, 'Would you lock all these doors, please, and do it quickly.'

"She looked at me as though I'd lost my mind. She couldn't believe what was going on.... And so she locked them, and I took a position right there in front of that door, and [Walt] took one right beside... and there were just the two of us standing there, waiting for them when they came up....

"They came down the long second-floor corridor and turned into the corridor leading straight to the entrance to our library. They were marching in military cadence, two rows of four men with the commanding officer walking beside the front row, and they were carrying ammonia. That was what they had, in big cans. And they were in step, and all of a sudden, the fellow at the side said, 'Halt, one two.' Just military precision. I'd been in ROTC and we'd learned this procedure.... The leader just said, 'Dump it here.'

"And so they immediately dumped two or three pails full of this ammonia all over the floor, and the fumes started coming up. And so they never did come any further. So then they ran down the stairs and out the building and they were gone.... [We threw] several pails of water [on the ammonia] and it made an awful mess, but it stopped the poisonous fumes."

Matters came to a head during the afternoon of Thursday, March 26, after the president of the Student Council told Dean Bond that an exam would be disrupted. "He said, 'We've talked about it in the council, and we think that this will be ugly. We know how the

II. LEGENDARY PROFESSORS

Business School students feel. They are out of patience with this disruption. They don't like it. And if they disrupt this examination, when all of them are in there together, I think there is going to be a battle.'"

The students wanted the exam canceled because "we were going to have violence." The school's Executive Committee concurred, canceled classes, and sent staff home. The deans met with President Fleming on Sunday, when Dean Bond and Law School Dean Frank Allen persuaded the other deans that the university should open on Monday.

It did open—with the assistance of four hundred and fifty plainclothes police. In a memo to faculty that morning, Dean Bond noted that "BAM representatives [agreed] to limit their activities to peaceful picketing *outside* University buildings [emphasis in original]. I would appreciate it if faculty members would move through the corridors . . . casually but frequently . . . to see that things are going satisfactorily. Our students are most anxious to make up for lost time and to pursue their educational objectives with vigor. Let's not disappoint them!"

Conclusion of the Strike

The BAM strike concluded on April 1, 1970, when the university agreed to provide funding to make it possible for 10 percent African American enrollment. The day before, the business school faculty endorsed the resolution: "The Executive Committee supports the University program to achieve a Black enrollment of 10 percent by 1973–74. . . . The Executive Committee . . . urges that all necessary steps including police, or military protection if required, be taken to protect academic freedom, personal life and property, and to reestablish and maintain the normal operations of the university."

Thankfully, the university did not have to ask for military protection. One month after the conclusion of the strike, the Ohio National Guard killed four unarmed students and wounded nine

8. Al Edwards

others protesting against the Vietnam War in what became known as the Kent State Massacre.

Vice President Spiro Agnew criticized the university's agreement to settle the strike, calling it a "surrender" and a "callow retreat from reality." He later resigned after pleading no contest to a felony charge of tax evasion and was replaced by Michigan graduate Gerald Ford.

Although the business school ramped up its earlier efforts to recruit African American students, by Fall Term 1973 only nineteen BBA and twenty-two graduate students were enrolled. As Dean Bond reported to the Regents in May 1973, African American students felt "they would be discriminated against in business, and it was therefore better to pursue graduate education in other fields."

The dean recognized the importance of hiring an African American faculty member, which the school had never done, and he found an ideal candidate in Al Edwards. In Dean Bond's words, he was an "economist of stature" who was also well-qualified to fill the school's need for a research director.

Figure 8.1. Al Edwards

Alfred Edwards's Biography

Education

- Attended a segregated high school in Key West, Florida, with fifteen classmates—seven of whom graduated
- Livingston College, BA *magna cum laude,* 1948
- University of Michigan, MA in Economics, 1949
- University of Iowa, PhD in Economics, 1958

Personal Background

- Born August 9, 1920, in Key West, Florida
- Died on January 26, 2007, in Ann Arbor, Michigan
- Married to Willie Mae Edwards
- Children Beryl and Alfred, Jr.

Professional Experience

- Worked in an aspirin factory in New York City before attending college
- US Army
- Taught at Southern University before enrolling in PhD program
- Taught at Michigan State University after completing PhD
- Part of a team on a two-year project to start the University of Nigeria at Nsukka

8. Al Edwards

- US Department of Agriculture, Deputy Assistant Secretary (under Presidents Kennedy, Johnson, and Nixon)
- Taught at Howard University
- US Consumer Product Safety Commission, Special Assistant to the Commissioner
- University of Michigan, Ross School of Business, Professor of Business Administration and Director of Research (retired 1990)
- Western Michigan University, Chair, Board of Trustees
- Security Bank Corporation, Board of Directors
- National Economic Association, President

Honors and Awards

- US Department of Agriculture, Distinguished Service Award
- University of Michigan, Alfred L. Edwards Collegiate Professorship
- National Black MBA Association, Distinguished Professor Award
- Black Business Student Association, Annual Alfred L. Edwards Conference
- Black Business Alumni Association, Alfred L. Edwards Scholarship
- National Economic Association, Alfred Edwards Award (for distinguished service)

II. Legendary Professors

Listen and Encourage

Known to students as "Dr. E," Al Edwards possessed two skills that mark great professors and leaders: the ability to listen to and encourage others. In using these skills, Al felt he was paying back those who had helped him earlier in life, such as the principal at his segregated high school who "guided me, and made sure that I was studying and doing all the right things."

The minister at Al's church was also influential. According to Al, the minister "took me under his wing and provided me with guidance and support." Inspired by these role models and his professors, Al became, in the words of Cecil Shepherd, president of the Ross Alumni Club of New York, the "Dean of Inspiration" to his students.

I witnessed Al's skills when walking past his office on my way to class. The office was often packed with students. As Al later noted, "Because I was the only African American faculty member here, the Black students naturally gravitated to me, you see. So they'd come in and talk with me all the time. Sometimes, it was nothing else, just to talk because they wanted to have a feeling of belonging and knowing somebody in the School, and that's how I began this rapport with the African American students in the Business School."

Even after his retirement, Al modestly noted, students "just want to come in and talk. So I just sit down and listen. That was so important to them to talk."

Through his listening skills, Al learned that African American students "felt, in a sense, rather isolated. The way it worked in the classroom was that there would be one black student in a class of 40, and they'd feel not as comfortable as they should be.... For example, I had African American students come in and talk to me, and they would say that they'd hear in the halls, in essence, 'Well, you shouldn't be here.'"

Al also learned that some students were treated differently in class. "For example, a student came to see me and said that the professor would never call on her in the class. So I talked to the professor, and he said, 'Well, Al, I didn't want to embarrass the student.' He really had good intentions. And I said, 'Well call on her because she wants to be called on.'"

Al encouraged students as he listened to their concerns. "[T]hey would come in, not feeling sure whether they could succeed, and that stemmed from many reasons, as you would recognize. So it was, in a sense, my job to tell them that: 'You can do this sort of thing,' and to try to point them to resources, when they needed them, to get it done."

A Builder

Through his work with students, Al recognized the need for organizational support in recruiting and supporting students at all levels. Due to his leadership, Michigan became involved in programs designed to recruit students for the undergraduate, MBA, and PhD programs and support students after their admission.

High School Recruitment: LEAD. High school students were encouraged to attend the LEAD program, which Al brought to the business school in 1981. The program motivated talented African American high school seniors, who might otherwise attend law school or medical school, to consider business education.

While on campus, students heard presentations by faculty members, experienced the case method, and visited various companies. As Al put it, students learned "what it really means to work in corporate America, because, frankly, the youngsters, at the time when you talk to them about business, they thought of being a teller in a bank or a salesperson or something like that. Those aren't bad jobs, but these kids were very talented, and therefore would say, 'Well, I'd rather be a doctor than to be a teller.'"

II. Legendary Professors

Today, Michigan Ross has several programs for high school students. For example, MREACH brings to campus sophomores and juniors from underrepresented groups and lower socioeconomic standing for sessions on academic and career preparation.

MBA Recruitment: Consortium for Graduate Study in Management. Through Al's encouragement, the business school joined six other schools in a Consortium for Graduate Study in Management, whose mission is to increase the number of African Americans, Hispanic Americans, and Native Americans in business schools and global management.

The Consortium awards full-tuition, merit-based fellowships that enable students to attend MBA programs at member schools. Judith Goodman, an assistant dean Al recruited to the school, served on the Consortium Board and played an influential role in the organization's success.

As a result of the Consortium, the student body became more diverse, making the business school more attractive to companies that had not previously recruited at the school. The school's success in attracting minority students encouraged peer schools to become more inclusive. Berkeley, Chicago, Columbia, Northwestern, Stanford, Yale, and a dozen other schools eventually joined Michigan and the other early members of the Consortium.

PhD Recruitment: Minority Summer Institute. Al played a vital role in the selection of the business school for the national Minority Summer Institute (MSI), which was based at the business school from 1990–93. Sponsored by the Association to Advance Collegiate Schools of Business (AACSB) and the Graduate Management Admission Council (GMAC), the Institute was designed to encourage African American, Hispanic, and Native American college students to enroll in PhD programs at business schools. At the time, 28 percent of college-age students were from those groups, but less than 3 percent of business school professors.

8. Al Edwards

The talented students admitted to the MSI program from around the country majored in various disciplines. While on campus for six weeks during the summer, they took intense PhD-type courses that introduced them to research methods. They also attended seminars where they met doctoral program directors and minority faculty members from around the country.

I served as director of the Institute and relied heavily on Al for advice. I was also grateful for the opportunity to work with a married couple who later became academic stars, David and Lynn Wooten. PhD students at the time, they served as teaching assistants in the program. Al had recruited them to Michigan, and they met in his office.

It was evident from the start that David and Lynn were destined for leadership roles. David is the Alfred L. Edwards Collegiate Professor at Michigan, where he has held numerous leadership positions, including associate dean at Michigan Ross. Lynn, too, has had a remarkable journey, serving as associate dean at the school before becoming dean at the Dyson School of Applied Economics and Management at Cornell. She is currently the president of Simmons University. Lynn and David have served as leaders in national professional organizations and have had outstanding success in teaching and research. Lynn's latest book, *The Prepared Leader*, coauthored by Wharton dean Erika James, has been widely praised by prominent business leaders.

A review conducted seven years after MSI ended indicated that at least thirty-seven of the 137 participating students (including two Rhodes Scholars) had applied to PhD programs, and fifteen had already graduated. An email from Ian Williamson, currently dean at the University of California-Irving's Merage School of Business, noted, "The experience I had in 1993 at MSI truly changed my life. I would have never considered becoming a professor without that program." Former GMAC President Dave Wilson concluded, "When one thinks about changing the world, the MSI initiative must be seen as a resounding success."

However, a new model was needed to reach a larger audience, including graduates in the workforce for a while. Fortunately, as Al noted, there was now "another group, called the PhD Project, which is really, in a sense, taking its [MSI's] place, but it's a different approach." The PhD Project was created in 1994 under the leadership of Bernie Milano, president of the KPMG Foundation, and has significantly increased the number of minority PhDs in business.

Support for Admitted Students: Black Business Student Association. When naming Al as a professor emeritus, the Michigan Board of Regents made special mention of his work as advisor of the Black Business Student Association (BBSA): "Professor Edwards helped the group to become one of the school's most productive student organizations."

Al described the evolution of BBSA's success by noting that the goal was "to help people do well.... That was the overall objective. But the secondary objective was to give them a social outlet, so they would have a party every once in a while.... And then they moved on to the point where they were going to help the students with job assignments-positions [by creating a resume book]. And then they decided that they would have an annual conference.... And then they opened up a scholarship program.... [And then they] sponsored an all-day Business Awareness Day for high school students."

A Role Model to All

As the first African American professor at the business school, Al Edwards was a trailblazer who paved the way for other minority faculty who followed. Remarkably, he successfully recruited and mentored students while meeting the same teaching and research demands facing other faculty. The service claims on the time of minority faculty members like Al can be extraordinary. I often observed Al working in his office late at night to make up for the many hours spent during the day supporting students.

In addition to his other responsibilities, Al was a personal role model to me and other faculty. Although we both arrived at the business school in 1974, Al was twenty-five years older and had substantial experience in universities, government, and business. At the university and at the church we attended, I benefitted from Al's advice on diverse professional and personal topics, ranging from book publishing to tips on organizing my tax records. I agree with former Dean Bob Dolan's comment about Al: "I am happy that I can count myself among the many 'students' who owe him a great deal of gratitude for the life lessons he taught."

UM Leadership Role of Frank Yates

Other minority faculty members who followed Al at Michigan Ross also served as role models for students and colleagues. One of them, Frank Yates, deserves special mention for his prominent leadership role in the university. Frank had a joint appointment in the Psychology Department and Michigan Ross and held a Thurnau professorship in recognition of his teaching excellence.

Highly respected for his research on cognitive processes in decision making, Frank published over one hundred books and articles. He received many awards recognizing the high quality of his work, including election to the American Academy of Arts and Sciences.

Frank achieved teaching and research success while creating and leading programs for minority students and taking on an unusually high number of service assignments. Shortly before he passed away in 2020, his CV indicated that he accepted around thirty significant administrative assignments at the University of Michigan and another three dozen professional service appointments.

Frank's efforts to help students began when, as a doctoral student at Michigan, he started a program now known as the Comprehensive Studies Program that helps students develop the skills needed for academic success. After Frank became a professor at the business school, he created the Preparation Initiative to help students interested in applying to the school develop the same skills. This program is designed for (but not limited to) minority students with potential for business leadership.

My involvement with Frank originated during my sabbatical as a visiting fellow at Cambridge University. During this leave, I became interested in decision analysis as it relates to the law, especially using decision trees to facilitate communication between business leaders and lawyers.

After returning to Michigan's campus, I wanted to learn more about behavioral decision-making research and discovered that Frank had an international reputation in the field. I attended his graduate course on decision making, and he became my guru in guiding me through the relevant literature. We also submitted a proposal for a National Science Foundation grant to support research on legal decision making, and I taught an annual session on "the role of business law in thriving businesses" in Frank's Preparation Initiative course.

A Triple Benefit for Michigan. Later, when I served as associate dean at the business school, I played a role in encouraging Frank to remain at Michigan and teach at the business school. In June 1997, I spoke with Tom Dunfee, a long-time friend who was Vice Dean at Wharton. I was surprised to learn from Tom that Wharton was on the verge of hiring Frank. I immediately met with Frank, who told me about his interests in teaching a course on business decision making and in creating a university-wide consortium on decision processes.

I immediately discussed these interests with Dean Joe White and Psychology Chair Pat Gurin. By August, which was warp speed compared with normal university processes, we had crafted a package satisfactory to Frank and provided a triple win for Michigan. First, Michigan Ross students benefitted from Frank's decision-making course in the business school. Second, faculty benefitted from the creation of a Decision Consortium that eventually included 140 faculty members from around the university. We met weekly to discuss research developments and listen to speakers responding to Frank's opening question, "What's keeping you up at night?" Third, the university retained a colleague who added immensely to its stature.

One irony in Frank's appointment at Michigan Ross, a school targeted during the 1970 BAM strike, is that as a graduate student, he drafted two proposals that were part of the student demands. One called for creating a program of instruction and research focused on African Americans, and the other for an academic success program for African American students.

When the strike ended, the Regents funded the proposals. The second proposal eventually resulted in the creation of the Comprehensive Studies Program (CSP). Today, CSP includes historically underrepresented students at the university, those from small high schools, and first-generation college students.

Reaching the Shore

An African American colleague at the business school once told me that being a member of a minority group was like swimming in an ocean, attempting to reach shore. He said that in the past, people would push you away from the beach through discriminatory laws and practices. Today, while you aren't prevented from reaching the shore, relatively few people attempt to help you reach land.

Al Edwards and faculty members who have followed him, like Frank Yates, are among those who, while helping minority faculty and students onto the shore, have created opportunities that benefit the entire university community. As Al said, "We must make sure that the doors that were opened for us do not become closed doors for others."

Chapter 9

CK Prahalad: The World's Most Influential Thinker

ON FEBRUARY 13, 2008, I conducted a seminar for the Mahratta Chamber of Commerce in Pune, India. Then, I traveled to the ICICI Bank Learning Center in Khandala, where I was scheduled to teach in the Michigan Ross Global Program for Management Development. Executives from India's leading companies were attracted to the program by the opportunity to learn from my colleague CK Prahalad, whom I would be meeting in Khandala.

During the ride to Khandala, my thoughts of CK triggered mixed emotions. I especially enjoyed his stories about business leaders, wine (he had an extensive collection, and his knowledge of wine could put a sommelier to shame), and art (he had a world-class collection). And I thought about CK's impact on the business world as a thought leader and consultant. For instance, during a previous trip to India to attend the wedding of one of my students in Mumbai, I met with Indian executives who provided examples of the impact his advice had on their business success.

But I also braced myself for the suggestions CK would inevitably provide for improving Michigan Ross. Because (with my colleague Ray Reilly) I headed our flagship Executive Program for senior executives, he viewed me as a sounding board for his ideas.

For instance, CK once sent me a memorandum shortly after we

finished the program. His basic theme was that the program had been great, but we needed immediate improvements to maintain our leadership position. He provided four pages of data with several tables and a three-page game plan that listed details of the next steps. This memo challenging the school to improve continually was classic CK in action!

Challenging the University and India

CK's obsession with striving for improvement was not limited to Michigan Ross or the companies seeking his advice. In a speech at the inauguration of University of Michigan President Mary Sue Coleman in 2003, he challenged the university to expand its view of the world: "One way for the University of Michigan to differentiate itself from other great universities is to provide access to high-quality education to a large number of people at low cost in a way that is sustainable and profitable. To achieve this goal, a different, high-technology solution is needed."

Michigan's leaders must have paid attention because the university soon created the Center for Academic Innovation, which offers open, online courses at low cost to learners worldwide. By 2024, over 11 million learners worldwide participated in these courses.

CK also challenged India, where he was born, during a celebration of the country's sixty years of independence. Instead of looking backward at the past sixty years, CK used the opportunity to look forward to the country's 75th year. He developed a plan based on "economic strength, technological vitality and moral leadership" that the Confederation of Indian Industry developed into a national vision document called India@75—The People's Agenda.

The Oscar of Management Thinking

In conversations with CK, I felt thankful that one of the outstanding thought leaders of all time was willing to focus on the success of

Michigan Ross. Every other year, Thinkers50 announces its ranking of the leading management thinkers in the world, which the *Financial Times* calls the "Oscars of management thinking." During the last two rankings (2007 and 2009) before he passed away, CK was named the leading management thinker in the world—ahead of the likes of Bill Gates, Malcolm Gladwell, Steve Jobs, Richard Branson, and Michael Porter. (Two Michigan Ross PhD program graduates, Chan Kim and Gary Hamel, ranked in the top ten both years, and another faculty member, Dave Ulrich, was in the top fifty.)

The other top thinkers respected CK. For example, Adi Ignatius, editor-in-chief of the *Harvard Business Review*, once organized a panel discussion and asked panelist Bill Gates "whom he most wanted with him on the panel." Gates responded, "CK Pralahad, the brilliant strategy thinker at the University of Michigan."

Howard Handler, one of CK's former MBA students and later an officer at Virgin Mobile, described a dinner where Richard Branson arrived with CK. "Just a couple of months before, I made everyone at Virgin Unite buy and read *The Fortune at the Bottom of the Pyramid*, and now CK was standing right in front of me with Richard, two of my business heroes!! I said, 'Dr. Prahalad?' Richard immediately asked, 'How do you know CK?' I said, 'I knew him before you, Richard, he was my professor!' We had some laughs and a great evening."

If CK had not passed away in 2010 at the age of sixty-eight, he would likely have dominated the ranking for years to come. In terms of accomplishments and joie de vivre, CK packed at least two lifetimes into his sixty-eight years. In terms of impact, he is still with us today.

Figure 9.1. CK Prahalad

CK Prahalad's Biography

Personal

- Born August 8, 1941, in Coimbatore, India; passed away April 16, 2010, in San Diego, California

- Wife Gayatri, son Murali, and daughter Deepa

Education

- Loyola College, BSc in physics (1960)

- Indian Institute of Management, MBA (1966)

- Harvard Business School, Doctor of Business Administration (1975)

II. LEGENDARY PROFESSORS

Professional Experience

- Union Carbide (1962–64)
- India Pistons (1966–71)
- Indian Institute of Management (1971–72)
- University of Michigan (1977–2010)
- Co-founder and CEO, Praja, Inc. (2000–2002)
- Consulting: Ahlstrom, AT&T, Cargill, Colgate-Palmolive, Honeywell, Oracle, Philips, TRW, and Unilever (and many others)
- Board Memberships: Hindustan Lever Ltd., NCR Corp., Pearson PLC, World Resources Institute (among others)

Selected Honors and Awards (among many)

- Padma Bhushan—one of India's highest civilian awards
- Honorary doctorates: University of London, University of Abertay-Dundee, Stevens Institute of Technology, and University of Tilburg
- Best Teacher Award, Michigan Ross
- Harvey C. Fruehauf Professor of Business Administration, University of Michigan
- Paul and Ruth McCracken Distinguished University Professor of Corporate Strategy, University of Michigan
- Lal Bahadur Sastri Award for Excellence in Management
- CK Prahalad Award for Scholarly Impact on Practice, Strate-

gic Management Society

- CK Prahalad Initiative, Michigan Ross
- William Davidson Institute Distinguished Fellow
- McKinsey Prize for best article, *Harvard Business Review* (four times)
- Faculty Pioneer Lifetime Award, Aspen Institute
- Italian Telecom Prize for Leadership in Business and Economic Thinking

Media Comments on CK's Passing

The New York Times: "His work on poverty, and earlier on how companies should build 'core competence,' earned him a loyal following in corporate boardrooms around the world."

The Economist: CK "was the most creative management thinker of his generation."

Time: "Long recognized as one of the world's foremost management thinkers, C.K. Prahalad was admired as much for his humanity as for his ideas on corporate strategy."

Financial Times: "Over the last three decades CK launched radical new ideas which would soon become conventional wisdom.... More than any other figure, he has provided a manifesto for how global business might prosper."

Publications

CK published many award-winning articles and books that were international bestsellers. In *The Palgrave Encyclopedia of Strategic Management* (August 18, 2016), Vijay Govindarajan, the Coxe

II. LEGENDARY PROFESSORS

Distinguished Professor at Dartmouth Tuck, explained the "three distinguishing characteristics in CK's scholarly contributions. First, CK opened up new fields instead of exploiting the same concept throughout his career. . . . Second, he was a contrarian thinker. His work is full of counter-intuitive insights and fresh thinking. Third, CK had a strong bias towards managerial action."

Because he was contrarian, CK's early research was not always accepted immediately. A paper he coauthored with Richard Bettis on dominant logic was rejected for eighteen months before it was finally accepted for publication by the *Strategic Management Journal* (SMJ). The paper later received the first SMJ Best Paper Prize and was selected as the best paper published over the past decade.

CK's five best-known books are:

- *The Multinational Mission* (with Yves Doz, 1987)

- *Competing for the Future* (with Gary Hamel, 1994)

- *The Future of Competition* (with Venkat Ramaswamy, 2004)

- *The Fortune at the Bottom of the Pyramid* (2004)

- *The New Age of Innovation* (with MS Krishnan, 2008)

Through his books and articles, CK created the language that shapes business strategy. Which ideas have had the most significant impact? He answered this question in an interview published in *strategy+business* (August 9, 2010). "One would be the idea of core competencies in a corporation. . . . Others include the bottom of the pyramid [the profitability in targeting the 2.5 billion people who make less than US$2.50 per day], co-creation [companies and customers innovating together], constrained innovation [typically used to develop very low-cost but functionally sophisticated products, like the Tata Nano], and dominant logic [the idea that companies are held back by their prevailing view of how to conduct business]."

Impact on Business Leaders

CK's ideas were influential in the business community, and he also walked the talk as he was in high demand worldwide as a consultant and served on several boards of directors. According to Mark Hurd when he was CEO of Hewlett-Packard, "The best way to describe CK is, he's an out-of-the-box guy who is pragmatic."

The Hurd quote is from an article in *Business Week* (January 23, 2006) titled "Business Prophet: How C.K. Prahalad is Changing the Way CEOs Think." The article described a consulting tactic he used during a weekend with leaders at the Dutch multinational company Philips. He started the meeting by reading an article that had just appeared in the *Financial Times* indicating that the company was going bankrupt. The article noted that the financial community wanted to know the company's game plan.

CK then told the leaders to "Forget what we are supposed to talk about. There is a major crisis. You had better figure out what you are going to do about it." The article states, "He then broke the stunned executives into two groups. They returned several hours later with ideas for radical restructuring involving up to 50,000 layoffs. Then Prahalad admitted he made the article up."

When advising companies, one of CK's favorite metaphors was that of a leader as a sheepdog rather than a shepherd. "A sheep dog has to respect some rules. Number one, you always lead from behind. Number two, you can bark a lot, but don't bite. And number three: don't lose any sheep."

Impact on Faculty

CK supported, encouraged, and inspired other faculty members through joint research and teaching. His Michigan Ross colleague Stuart Hart (with whom CK worked on the bottom of the pyramid concept) commented, "When I was struggling to define my professional identity, CK was one of the few faculty colleagues who

II. LEGENDARY PROFESSORS

encouraged me to pursue my personal passion about the connection between business and the environment. In fact, were it not for CK, I never would have made the conscious decision (which I did in 1990) to devote the rest of my professional life to sustainable enterprise. That was the *best decision I ever made*. [Emphasis in original.]"

Another colleague, Ted London, noted how CK supported his research: "CK was an extraordinary scholar. He helped us think about the poor in completely different ways—took old, intractable problems, and thought about them in a new way. He didn't have to own the idea; rather, he was willing to put the idea forward and work with others to advance them and move them forward. He was incredibly generous."

CK's presence contributed to the collaborative community at Michigan Ross. For example, Executive Program faculty often sat in on each other's classes so that we could link our teaching to topics in different courses. I benefitted from observing CK's teaching skills. Learning about his views on strategy enabled me to clarify my work on law as a source of competitive advantage.

I also benefited from CK's consulting contacts. One of his clients was Cargill, the largest privately owned company in the United States. Through CK, I got to know the CEO, Ernie Micek, and enjoyed our discussions about whether managing a business with several generations of family ownership was more challenging than leading a company with publicly traded stock.

I also enjoyed meeting Cargill leaders in social settings, although the dialog was quite different from my usual academic conversations. For instance, over dinner one evening, the wife of one of the company's owners told me about a birthday gift she had just received from her husband: part ownership of the Minnesota Vikings football team.

Impact on Students: What About Bob?

CK was a role model for anyone who is a teacher, including business leaders who must teach subordinates about the requirements for business success. Here is a mini-case study to test your teaching potential.

A team of students in CK's course wanted to kick "Bob" (who was strong in finance) off the team because he contributed nothing to the team's efforts and didn't even attend team meetings. The students' entire grade depended on their team project, and they all would receive the same grade. They went to CK's office to ask permission to remove Bob from the team. If you were in CK's shoes, what would you do?

According to one of the students, Michigan Ross graduate Rebecca Cooper, CK "tented his fingers and turned toward the window as the sky darkened and a few flakes of snow drifted onto the sill. 'I am not inclined to let you force Bob out of the group. . . . As you know, I come from India and there we believe that it is our responsibility to help those who need it.'"

When the team members protested that it was unfair to help Bob because he wasn't making any effort, CK responded, "This is his karma and it will even itself out somewhere in his life. It is not for us to say when."

While initially upset with this decision, Rebecca reported that "The lessons from my favorite professor were manifold. I discovered how strong I was in finance when another team member and I were forced to run the numbers after Bob dropped out. I learned that things are not always fair. . . . Rather than focusing on our resentment, CK had turned us back toward the goal. How we felt about Bob didn't matter. He didn't or couldn't or wouldn't show up. That was our reality. It was how we chose to deal with it that mattered."

CK especially enjoyed action-based learning, the signature feature of the Michigan Ross experience. With this approach, students

II. Legendary Professors

apply what they have learned in the classroom to real-world situations through multidisciplinary action projects (MAP) worldwide.

Like other faculty members, CK used this experience to co-create knowledge with his students. His former student Sachin Rao describes his MAP project: "Under CK's guidance, I studied and documented break-through models for rural distribution being developed by agribusiness companies in India. I look upon my work with CK as the defining event of my Michigan experience. . . . CK's presence, on a professional and personal plane, had a lot to do with the enduring impact of the experience."

Here is a sampling of other students' comments about CK:

- "[W]e completely adored him and so we asked for more of his time. He generously agreed to create a strategy course that was held on Saturdays. I believe he would often fly all night from his consulting jobs in foreign countries to make our Saturday lectures. Those lectures were some of the most enthralling moments of my life. Dr. Prahalad would tirelessly lecture for several hours often with no sleep and without a break as I speedily took notes." Greg Jones, MBA 1997

- "Fifteen years after graduating from Michigan I was in the international lounge at the airport waiting for a flight to Beijing. I saw CK from across the room and wanted to say hello. As I walked over, CK looked up and said, 'Hi Jon. How are you doing?' I was amazed that after all the years and the hundreds of students that CK had taught that he recognized me immediately." Jon Maples, MBA 1985

- "I will never forget the advice CK gave us students during that semester, even though it was over 30 years ago. He said that we were gifted with abilities and credentials. It bothered him when he saw people like that take the easy road and go work for some large and highly successful company. He said those companies don't need you as much and they won't challenge you as much. Instead, he implored us to go work for the smaller companies or the companies who were going through difficulties. Those are the places where you will stretch yourself and make greater contributions. He wanted us to prove our worth and make a difference." Gerald Nanninga, MBA 1978

Students also recalled their favorite CK quotes years after graduation. Here are examples:

- "Make a difference in the world."

- "Leadership is about having a point of view about the future, and leadership is about hope."

- "We are all sons and daughters of Adam. . . . Our diverse cultural expressions collectively testify to the excellence of our common creator."

- "The business school is not a sausage factory for corporate America. There is no such thing as a sexy business. Janitorial services, furniture making and meat packing can be as exciting as alternate fuel development or spacecraft design."

- "Strategy is simple, it's basic, it's so obvious that it's often in your face—which is why it's so easy to not see it."

- "Above all else, be true to your family and loved ones."

CK's Values

CK's lessons to students were value-laden. Former student Nina Henning observed, "In 2007, I found myself in CK's classroom for the first time and quickly came to realize that his agenda for his students was much broader than teaching us about the 'bottom of the

II. Legendary Professors

pyramid.' He was determined to give us enduring lessons about moral leadership."

Every year, CK closed his courses with a summary of his values. In 2004, for the only time in thirty years, he had a scheduling conflict he could not avoid when teaching in the Executive Program. So, he sent me a video of his closing comments to share with the class. The comments were so powerful that a participant from the armed forces asked whether he could show the video to the Secretary of the Air Force so that he could recommend CK for a retreat with four-star generals.

Here is an edited summary of the comments, which can serve as a guide for leaders worldwide when faced with difficult decisions:

> I have been pushing you to come to terms with your own values because without a fundamental understanding of your own values and without being very self-aware, you cannot be activists and you cannot be agents of change. I now have an obligation to share with you what my values are.
>
> What is the meaning of being a responsible manager? The starting point for me is learning the importance of nonconformity and being a lonely thinker. Leaders have to understand the loneliness at the top. It is not easy. It is not always possible that when you lead, other people will immediately see where you are going. It takes time. Therefore it is important for leaders to understand how to be lonely and how to be nonconformists.
>
> The second most important point is that you cannot help other people if you're not very good yourself. Therefore take personal responsibility for continued excellence, continued intellectual excellence, financial excellence, and health—because if you're not healthy, you cannot help other people. If you're not intellectually oriented, if you're not better than others, you cannot help others. So the fundamental responsibility of a good manager,

and a good leader, is to take responsibility for personal excellence and ongoing excellence.

The third point is that all of us will have successes and failures. As leaders, we have to put humility into our success and certainly courage in failure, and both are equally important. If you lose humility, you lose the capacity to learn. If you don't have courage, you cannot continue to lead. So, we need to have humility in success and courage in failure.

We are now ready to take responsibility for the growth and the well-being of others around us. It's our job to make sure that we stretch each person to the limits of their capabilities, and that's an obligation that leaders have.

It's our job to make sure we have the ability to look at differences, respect all people, and assimilate differences. That is where the world will be a safer place. It is also important for us to recognize that people do not ask for favors. They ask for fairness, and therefore it is important to have the ability to focus on due process in large organizations to provide everybody a share of voice, to listen to people, and make sure that they're treated very fairly.

I believe that we have to think about loyalty as a multi-dimensional issue. Certainly, I expect to be loyal to the organization, loyal to my profession, and loyal to the communities in which I live and work, but most important is loyalty to the family. For me, that is very central. Without our families, our parents, our spouses and our children, we cannot achieve anything that we claim that we have achieved.

Management is an interesting profession. We as managers are the very privileged few. That is a privilege, but it's also the cross we will carry all our lives. With this privilege comes the obligation to serve. Therefore, I look at this opportunity and this position not just as privileges, but obligations, and I think we need to keep both of them in perspective. I would suggest that we match our learning with compassion and achievement with understanding. We as managers will not be judged by what we say we want to do, but people will judge us by what we do.

Summing Up an Extraordinary Life

How can one sum up the life and works of one of the greatest management thinkers in history? When someone asked him to describe India, CK referred to the story of the blind men who touched an elephant and then described the elephant based on the part they touched. Explaining a larger-than-life polymath like CK creates a similar experience because he impacted people in many different ways. In a book of remembrances published after he passed away, I attempted to summarize the various features of his life I had observed during the thirty-three years we taught together at Michigan Ross.

Here are my slightly edited comments from that book:

> As his colleague for many years, I was fortunate to witness many facets of CK Prahalad's life. There was **CK the teacher**, whose courses inspired MBA students and corporate executives to think beyond traditional boundaries and to convert their thoughts into action in a socially responsible manner. There was **CK the author**, who wrote best-selling books and award-winning articles in which he developed enduring concepts that have shaped the contours of corporate strategy. There was **CK the consultant**, who guided business executives worldwide when they faced complex strategic decisions involving significant corporate resource commitments. There was **CK the mentor**, who was generous with his time and wisdom in advising faculty colleagues and students. There was **CK the academic**,

whose thought-provoking research led to the development of new fields of scholarly inquiry.

There was **CK the entrepreneur**, who brought theory to practice in starting new ventures and who, as a social entrepreneur, searched for pragmatic ways to alleviate poverty and passionately encouraged others to do the same. There was **CK the philosopher and historian**, who could, for example, knowledgeably launch a corporate strategy course with a discussion of why business leaders should understand Cortez's defeat of Montezuma. There was **CK the loyalist**, who could have accepted a professorship at any university in the world but remained devoted to the University of Michigan, where he was an intense advocate for excellence in teaching and research at the Ross School of Business.

On a more personal level, there was **CK the raconteur**, who could mesmerize audiences in social and academic settings with stories often laced with humor and drawn from his multifaceted experiences. There was **CK the art enthusiast**, whose collection of Indian art was world class. There was **CK the friend**, who always had a cheerful greeting and smile, no matter how tired he was from his latest travels. Most importantly, there was **CK, the husband and father**, whose love for Gayatri, Murali, Deepa, and his grandchildren was a driving force and motivation for all his accomplishments.

CK's wife, Gayatri, deserves special mention. An article in *Forbes* emphasized her essential role in supporting and encouraging CK, including her travel to take care of him on trips where he was immersed in his hectic lifestyle.

Following CK's passing, the Prime Minister of India, Dr. Manmohan Singh, sent Gayatri a message offering his condolences. Later, at a memorial service, he observed, "Some people leave behind wealth, others leave behind some remnants of power, and some leave behind the passionate energy of their ideas that continually stimulate those whose lives they touch. CK Prahalad belonged to this third category."

Whenever I approached CK with a "How are you doing?" greeting, he would always reply with a twinkle in his eye, "I am surviving." CK will survive forever in our hearts and minds as his thoughts inspire those who want to improve the world. In a *Forbes* article, Nish Acharya (former Senior Advisor to the US Secretary of Commerce) observed, "Somewhere in the world today, a person is dedicating his or her life to a pressing social or political injustice that they believe must be corrected. They will fight discrimination, create solutions for clean drinking water, or push for legislation to provide quality education to young people. They will be inspired by Mahatma Gandhi, but read from the playbook of CK Prahalad."

PART III

BEYOND THE MICHIGAN ROSS CAMPUS: ANN ARBOR AND THE UNIVERSITY OF MICHIGAN

Chapter 10. The Best College Town and a Popular Student Hangout

Chapter 11. Michigan Ross Ties to Athletics Within a World-Renowned University

Chapter 10

The Best College Town and a Popular Student Hangout

WHEN SELECTING A place to teach and study, outstanding faculty and students look for more than a high-quality business school. They want a school located within a major university and a vibrant community. Michigan Ross, situated in a world-class university and a cosmopolitan city, meets these requirements. This chapter focuses on the city of Ann Arbor. The next chapter explores Michigan Ross's place within the University of Michigan.

This chapter opens with background on Ann Arbor and the collaboration between Michigan Ross and an iconic local business, Zingerman's. But Zingerman's isn't the only business that plays a significant role in the school's community. Casa Dominick's, a restaurant a few steps from Michigan Ross, is a meeting place for faculty, students, alumni, and townies. This chapter explains how this popular hangout became the birthplace of one of the world's largest companies and why its business model raises a question every business student should consider.

A trigger warning is appropriate before you read on. This chapter includes disturbing content that includes the drinking of blood. This should not cause concern if you visit campus—unless your blood type is O-negative!

III. Beyond the Michigan Ross Campus

Ann Arbor

Celebrating its 200th birthday in 2024, Ann Arbor is one hundred years older than the business school. A city of 120,000 located on the banks of the Huron River in Southeastern Michigan, Ann Arbor has a thriving arts and cultural environment, incredible dining and recreational opportunities, and a business culture described as a combination of Silicon Valley and Midwest values. Recent rankings by *Fortune*, *US News & World Report*, *WalletHub*, and others have concluded that Ann Arbor ranks No. 1 among the:

- best places to live for quality of life
- most educated cities in America
- best places to live for families
- best college towns and cities in America

    Close to a major international airport—Detroit Metro Airport—Ann Arbor is a gateway to the world. Michigan Ross students can fly to New York City, Chicago, or Washington, DC, for the day when working on action-learning projects or visiting companies recruiting them. One of my colleagues at the business school commutes weekly to Ann Arbor from New York City. She jokes, "It takes me fewer hours to get from my NYC apartment to Ann Arbor, Michigan, than going on the Long Island Railroad into Manhattan." Detroit Metro provides students easy access to Europe, Asia, and elsewhere when participating in global summer experiences, internships, and exchange programs.

10. The Best College Town and a Popular Student Hangout

Michigan Ross Collaboration with Ann Arbor Businesses

In addition to access to worldwide opportunities, Michigan Ross benefits from interacting with Ann Arbor's thriving business community. The school's partnership with the legendary business conglomerate Zingerman's is a notable example.

Known primarily for its delicatessen, which *Food & Wine* magazine has named the best deli in America (beating out well-known New York City delis), Zingerman's is a community of businesses that includes a restaurant, bakehouse, creamery, mail-order business, coffee company, training operation, catering services, and candy company. The deli is the jewel in this crown of enterprises. Among its tasty specialties is the Reuben sandwich that President Obama enjoyed during a visit.

Students don't have to leave the Michigan Ross campus to enjoy Zingerman's deli menu. A Zingerman's café, Seven10East, is located on the east side of the school. The cafe serves coffee, smoothies, pastries, sandwiches, and salads.

Students can also engage in team-building at Zingerman's picturesque Cornman Farms, learn how the company became successful through classroom visits by the founders, and analyze its business model through studies like Professor Wayne Baker's case on its open-book finance system. Faculty have also worked with Zingerman's to develop its positive work environment.

The Ultimate College Hangout

While students benefit from formal collaborations between Michigan Ross and businesses like Zingerman's, they are also consumers of world-class goods and services offered by local businesses. A prime example is Casa Dominick's. During my experience as a visiting professor at Berkeley, Harvard, Stanford, and elsewhere, I have not discovered a better college hangout. Of particular interest

III. Beyond the Michigan Ross Campus

to business school students is Dominick's role in creating one of the world's most successful multinational corporations.

Figure 10.1. Dominick's entrance

A Walking Tour to Dominick's. Your visit to Dominick's from the business school begins at the main entrance on the west side of the Michigan Ross campus. You walk north on Tappan Street past a sixty-five-foot, 250-year-old bur oak that was moved one hundred yards at a cost of $400,000 during expansion of the main business school building in 2014. A short walk west on Monroe Street then brings you to your destination—812 Monroe Street—and Dominick's welcoming patio.

While sitting on the patio, you are treated to an incredible architectural achievement: the University of Michigan Law Quadrangle. The quadrangle was a gift from Law School graduate and New York

10. The Best College Town and a Popular Student Hangout

City attorney William Cook. Cook never saw the result of his gift, as he died before it was completed.

The Quad is modeled after buildings at Cambridge and Oxford, and you will quickly see the resemblance as you look at the Law School library across the street from Dominick's. The view will remind you of the "Backs" at Cambridge—a grassy area backing up to the River Cam—where visitors can view fifteenth-century King's College Chapel. A poll conducted by the American Institute of Architects concluded that the Law School library is one of the top one hundred buildings in America.

Founding of Dominick's. As you move from the reverie of England at the front patio of Dominick's to a courtyard in the back, you will stop in a room where you can order food and drink. In past years, you first had to pass a human guard dog named Silvio to enter.

The cousin of Dominick's founder Dominick DeVarti, Silvio emigrated from a small town in Italy in the mid-1950s. In Ann Arbor, he started a tile company and completed the beautiful tile work that adorns the walls at Dominick's. With a deep scowl, Silvio was a scary presence to many students when he demanded to see their IDs. Before he passed away, he had a devoted following of alumni who loved to visit with him on their campus visits.

Once you clear the ID hurdle, you enter the room where you can place your order. The walls are covered with photos and posters that depict local political and cultural events, such as the 1971 John Sinclair Freedom Rally. Well-known New York City-based performance artist Pat Oleszko, pictured on one wall, calls Dominick's a museum that serves food.

Most days, Dominick's owner Rich DeVarti oversees operations from a corner of the room where he greets customers. During a recent visit, I chatted with Rich's wife and her ninety-four-year-old mother from China, who were sitting nearby. During another visit, an Ann Arbor Rowing Club member stopped by to ask Rich for a donation. Rich reminded him that one of the club's boats carries his father's name, Dominick DeVarti.

Dominick started the restaurant in 1959. His parents emigrated from a small village in Italy and settled on the east coast, where Dominick was born. A friend persuaded young Dominick to enlist in the Army Air Corps so they could attend college on the GI Bill. During World War II, he was a bombardier and navigator on planes that bombed bridges near Remagen in Germany. After the war, the friend suggested that they should enroll at the University of Michigan.

After college, Dominick started several businesses, including pizzerias, and ran unsuccessfully for mayor of Ann Arbor. In 1959, he acquired the property on Monroe Street, which had previously been a grocery store and sandwich shop, and started the restaurant. Over the years, Dominick acquired five additional buildings in the area, one of which was incorporated into the restaurant when he expanded the original building. In 2024, the University of Michigan purchased two neighboring houses for $3.8 million.

After Dominick's passing, Rich became the owner. A modest, soft-spoken individual, seventy-year-old Rich has continued to improve the restaurant. Like his father, he takes a personal interest in customers. During a recent visit, I ate at the restaurant with my long-time friend, Michigan finance professor Han Kim. Although Han had not eaten there recently, Rich remembered to include his favorite hot peppers with the order.

Rich is a father figure and friend to his staff, some of whom are second-generation employees. When I asked one of them what he thought of Rich, he replied, "Chill, laid-back, and personable. He's the most laid-back employer I've ever had. He also provides free beer after the restaurant closes."

Ann Arbor Film Festival. Photos and posters from the Ann Arbor Film Festival, the oldest experimental film festival in America, dominate the room where Rich sits. The film festival originated in

10. The Best College Town and a Popular Student Hangout

the early 1960s, during conversations at Dominick's.

George Manupelli, an art professor at the University of Michigan and a friend of Dominick, founded the festival and served as its director for many years. Prominent artists and directors like Brian De Palma, Andy Warhol, and George Lucas have exhibited at the festival.

Today, Dominick's welcomes filmmakers at the annual festival with a dinner for seventy people. An award at the festival honors University of Michigan graduate Lawrence Kasdan, who produced or co-wrote the *Star Wars* films, *Raiders of the Lost Ark*, and many other hits.

Another award honors noted filmmaker Ken Burns, who was Rich's classmate in elementary school in Ann Arbor and played on Dominick's little league baseball team. The DeVarti family sponsors two awards: the George Manupelli Founder's Spirit Award and the Prix DeVarti for Funniest Film. Prix DeVarti "recognizes the 60-year friendship between Dominick's pub and the AAFF."

Placing Your Order. The menus on the walls have a predominantly Italian theme, with variations of pasta, pizza, ravioli, and lasagna complemented by some exotic alternatives. My favorite non-Italian dish is Bung Sao, which has a curious history. Dominick once decided to run a traditional Italian restaurant with a sit-down service on the second floor. When that failed, the upstairs became a Vietnamese restaurant, which also failed.

One of the Vietnamese women, Mui Truong, stayed on, and she has taken my orders at Dominick's for over forty years. Her invention, Bung Sao (which, according to Google Translate, means "how about it"), is a healthy mixture of rice noodles, chicken, lettuce, peanuts, and fish sauce.

You can top off your meal with a creative dessert such as limoncello cheesecake or cannoli cake. Drinks include a variety of beers, wine, and mixed drinks. One of the most popular beers,

III. Beyond the Michigan Ross Campus

Oberon, has a Dominick's connection. Bell's Brewery originally called the beer Solsun, and the first tap was at Dominick's. After a trademark dispute, Bell's changed the name from Solsun to Oberon, the King of the Fairies in Shakespeare's *A Midsummer Night's Dream*.

The formula for one drink, Dominick's famous sangria, is secret. Rich is multilingual, and he studied Spanish at the University of Madrid before completing his undergraduate degree at the University of Michigan. He returned home with a novel recipe for sangria. Over the years, he refined the recipe, which is a hit with customers.

After paying for your order, you often receive change in $2 bills, Kennedy half dollars, and dollar coins. You can then bring your drinks, poured into mason canning jars, to the front patio facing the Cambridge-looking Law Quadrangle or to a garden courtyard in the back and wait for a loudspeaker announcement that your food is ready for pick up.

Garden Courtyard. The mellow sound of conversation interspersed with laughter makes the garden courtyard a welcoming destination. The courtyard transports you to what feels and looks like a small piazza in an Italian village. Tables and chairs surround a fountain set into a stone wall. At the top of the fountain stands a small statue of a naked boy urinating into the water—a copy of Manneken Pis, a symbol of Brussels. A covered walk leads to a pavilion at the back of the courtyard.

You will find a small table near the courtyard's entrance with a sign that says, "Reserved for Dominick Executive Committee and Invited Guests." From my student days in the 1960s, I remember Dominick sitting there like a feudal lord, greeting customers as they entered the courtyard.

Perhaps the most notable feature of the courtyard and elsewhere in the restaurant is what is missing: TVs and music. This is intentional. When Rich began to work at Dominick's in the fourth grade,

10. The Best College Town and a Popular Student Hangout

he loved listening to the conversations as he cleared the tables. As he puts it, "The conversation is the music." The music of conversation is provided by a melting pot of customers that reflect the diversity of Ann Arbor, including "Cookies" from a nearby all-women's dorm called Martha Cook, alumni, townies, athletes, and fraternity and sorority members.

Upper and Lower Levels. Dominick's second floor and lower level are used for special events. Events are announced by notices written on pizza boxes nailed to the wall at the entrance to Dominick's: "Bio Chem meets in the garden area all the way straight back in the area by the gazebo" or "Fidelity Happy Hour meets to the right at the center tables on the front patio west side."

When exploring the second floor, you will notice beautiful etched glass panels made in France in the 1800s. Because of its heavy weight, the glass was removed from the dome of the State Capitol building in Lansing in 1957 and later purchased by Dominick. In 1989, a dome restoration team visited the restaurant to study the panels before reproducing them.

The lower level is dark and eerie, making it a perfect setting for a vampire movie. Filmmaker Ed Shimborske selected this area as one of the sites when he filmed *On Gallows Hill* in 2023. A blend of horror and black comedy, the story has a unique twist: the film's vampires need their specific blood type to survive. Without type O-negative, the vampire hero will become a living corpse. He finds the required blood type through a job packaging blood for a coven of vampires in a basement—Dominick's lower level.

To say more would require a spoiler alert. A trailer for the film includes the street outside Dominick's and the basement. If scenes from the film disturb you, here is a secret that a Dominick's employee (an extra in the movie) shared: Dominick's famous sangria was used to create the "blood" swilled by vampires.

III. BEYOND THE MICHIGAN ROSS CAMPUS

The Birthplace of Domino's Pizza. Founder Dominick had many ties to the Ann Arbor business community, where he was a leader of a network of businesses that supported each other. There was the Blind Pig, a local watering hole and music venue where legends such as John Lennon and Jimi Hendrix played. At Washtenaw Dairy, you will find Michigan students and neighborhood families sitting outside on warm summer evenings, enjoying cones that combine enormous scoops of ice cream with low prices. Pizza Bob's is the home of world-famous chapatis.

Dominick's is the birthplace of another business, Domino's Pizza. The Domino's story began when Dominick acquired a pizza place in Ypsilanti, a town bordering Ann Arbor. Because the place was small, Dominick decided to deliver pizzas to customers via jeep. This proved a headache as customers called in fake orders, and criminals robbed drivers. The robberies were so common that Dominick fashioned a billy club—a bat with holes in it on a strap—so that drivers could protect themselves.

Given the challenges of pizza delivery, Dominick agreed to sell the business when he received an offer from two brothers, Tom and Jim Monaghan. They borrowed the $900 needed for the purchase. Rich remembers his father teaching the brothers how to make pizza sauce and dough in the kitchen at Dominick's. Tom, a University of Michigan dropout, later bought out his brother by giving him a VW Beetle they used to deliver pizzas.

Monaghan later changed the name of the Ypsilanti business to Domino's, which he liked because it was similar to Dominick's. This turned out to be a costly decision when the maker of Domino Sugar filed a lawsuit claiming trademark infringement. In 1980, following lengthy litigation, a federal appellate court decided that Domino's Pizza could continue using the name. Over dinner, Monaghan once told me that his litigation costs were around $400,000—roughly $1.5 million in today's dollars. He explained that his backup plan if they lost the case was to change the name to Pizza Express.

10. The Best College Town and a Popular Student Hangout

Using the pizza delivery model originated by Dominick, Monaghan established his reputation as a legendary American entrepreneur. Although he sold over 90 percent of Domino's to Bain Capital for around $1 billion when he retired in 1998, he still owns Domino's Farms Office Park in Ann Arbor, where the company's main office is located. Monaghan once owned the Detroit Tigers and founded Ave Maria University, among his other ventures.

While Monaghan was achieving spectacular financial success worldwide, Dominick spent his days at the table reserved for the Executive Committee in the lush courtyard at the back of his restaurant, listening to the conversation and laughter of generations of customers. Today, Rich spends most of his time sitting near the counter, where he can easily greet customers and interact with employees.

The Eternal Questions for Business Students. The contrast between Domino's and Dominick's business models raises challenging questions for business students. What is your goal in life? If your life span is, say, 2000–2080, how do you want to spend the time represented by the dash? Would you rather create the world's largest pizza company, worth around $18 billion today, or spend your working days immersed in the family atmosphere of a Dominick's-style restaurant? You decide: Domino's or Dominick's?

Rich's thoughts about this question are clear. When I asked him whether he or his father had any regrets about Monaghan's success following the sale of the Ypsilanti business, he replied without hesitation. "Our customers meet their spouses here while waiting in line. They have engagement parties and get married here. Second-generation employees work here. All this gives us pleasure. What we have here is precious."

Chapter 11

Michigan Ross Ties to Athletics Within a World-Renowned University

AT 2 A.M. ON OCTOBER 14, 1960, then-Senator John F. Kennedy addressed thousands of University of Michigan students from the steps of the Michigan Union. With these inspiring words, he launched the idea that came to be known as the Peace Corps:

> I want to express my thanks to you, as a graduate of the Michigan of the East, Harvard University. . . . How many of you who are going to be doctors, are willing to spend your days in Ghana? Technicians or engineers, how many of you are willing to work in the Foreign Service and spend your lives traveling around the world? On your willingness to do that, not merely to serve one year or two years in the service, but on your willingness to contribute part of your life to this country, I think will depend the answer whether a free society can compete. . . . [T]his University is not maintained by its alumni, or by the state, merely to help its graduates have an economic advantage in the life struggle. There is certainly a greater purpose, and I'm sure you recognize it.

11. Michigan Ross Ties to Athletics

Figure 11.1. JFK's Peace Corps speech at the Michigan Union

Focusing on JFK, students probably didn't notice two sculptures, still present, flanking him above the steps where he spoke. On one side is a sculpture known as "Athlete," a muscular student wearing shorts and a sleeveless T-shirt with a basketball, tennis racket, and baseball at his feet. He faces south toward the university's athletic campus.

On the other side is another sculpture, "Scholar," the same student wearing a tie and an academic gown. Holding a book in one hand and a mortarboard in the other, he gazes toward the central campus where the main classrooms are located. Created in 1918 by Michael Murphy, the sculptures are designed to represent the ideal Michigan student (at a time when the campus was male-oriented).

The sculptures symbolize the strong tie between scholarship and athletics at Michigan. This chapter provides examples of this link, using Michigan Ross as a case study.

In addition to its connections to athletics, the business school

III. Beyond the Michigan Ross Campus

benefits in other ways from its location in a world-class university. The following section provides examples before turning to athletics.

The University of Michigan and Michigan Ross: A Balance of Excellence

A profile at *Poets&Quants* opens by noting that Michigan Ross "rightfully believes that business can be an extraordinary vehicle for positive change in the world. Michigan Ross is at the heart of a renowned university and a welcoming college town." The "welcoming college town" is described in the previous chapter. Here, we examine the benefits of the school's position within a "renowned university."

In its 2023 "World Reputation Rankings," *Times Higher Education* listed Michigan as one of the top twenty universities in the world. As noted in Chapter 4, *Poets&Quants* ranks business schools by combining the five most influential and credible rankings. Five of the top ten business schools in this 2023–24 composite ranking are located within one of the top twenty universities worldwide: Columbia, Harvard, Michigan, Stanford, and Yale.

Leading universities adopt one of two fundamental approaches when establishing their reputations. Some universities focus their resources on selected areas. One result of this approach, mentioned by Berkeley history professor David Hollinger in his essay "Academic Culture at Michigan, 1938–1988," is a "'Chicago School' of this and a 'Chicago School' of that." Hollinger notes that Stanford achieved prominence by focusing resources on selected areas called "steeples."

The other approach, adopted by Michigan, is to achieve excellence by balancing resources among programs across the university. According to Hollinger, instead of "concentrating of resources in selected areas," the university has adopted a pluralistic tradition that has "sustained Michigan's overall greatness." This has produced a "capacity to inspire" that derives "from the enormous range of

11. Michigan Ross Ties to Athletics

learned pursuits and doctrines available here." In 2024, *US News and World Report* ranked an amazing 117 graduate programs at the university in the top ten.

Reflecting the university's balance of excellence, Michigan Ross offers students a balanced education through its specializations (accounting, finance, management, marketing, and so on). As noted in Chapter 4, commenting on the *US News* 2023–24 ranking of specializations, *Poets&Quants* (April 26, 2023) noted that "Only one school ranked in every one of *U.S. News'* 13 specialization categories: Michigan Ross School of Business. It's a feat the Ross School has now accomplished for three straight years."

The balance of excellence at Michigan Ross extends beyond academic specializations. *Princeton Review* ranks business schools using a variety of categories. In 2023, *Poets&Quants* analyzed this ranking based on what it considered the ten most important categories. While *P&Q* included some academic categories (such as finance, marketing, and management), business schools were also ranked based on who had the best professors, classroom experience, campus environment, and career prospects. Michigan (along with Virginia Darden and Duke Fuqua) was one of three schools that scored far better than other business schools in these categories.

In addition to benefitting from this balance of excellence within the business school, Michigan Ross students can enroll in over twenty dual degree programs that include environment and sustainability, information, public health, law, engineering, higher education, urban planning, and public policy.

They can also take courses throughout the university where they will interact with students from various disciplines. They might find themselves in a course with a student-athlete like Tom Brady or a future entertainer like Madonna. Or they might sit next to classmates destined to become CEOs or founders of companies like Boeing, the Buffalo Bills football team, Domino's Pizza, General Motors, Google, Groupon, H&R Block, Lockheed, and Skype. More CEOs from Fortune 1000 companies have graduated from Michigan than any other public university.

One CEO who graduated from Michigan Ross, Robert Isom at American Airlines, commented on the benefits of his balanced education: "What Michigan did for me is it brought everything together into all these different functions. How do they come together in a business? It seemed like every class was another piece of the puzzle being put together."

The Athletic Department

The Athletic Department, perhaps more than any other individual school or college at Michigan, plays a unifying role on campus. At the conclusion of the 1925–26 academic year, the first graduates of the business school listened to the commencement address by Sir Frederick Whyte at the football field. He emphasized that "in the University Union, in the gymnasium and on the football field [we learn] the value of cooperation; we learn the lesson of friendship; and at the end we carry with us a band of friends whose attachment is more precious than any other gift which the University has to offer."

As noted in Chapter 2, poet Robert Frost spent that year as a visiting fellow at Michigan. During a dinner party when he was on campus, Michigan President Marion Burton quipped that "Robert Frost may be even more popular than Football Coach Fielding Yost." Frost replied, "Let's put that to the test: schedule a reading for me at the same time as a home football game. More than 30,000 will be cheering at Ferry Field, but Hill Auditorium will be empty since even I will be at the game."

More recently, in 2013, the university adopted the famous Block M, long a symbol of Michigan athletics, as its logo after completing a branding survey. According to the president, Mary Sue Coleman, "It pays tribute to our collective heritage, allows us to speak in one voice, and helps us move into our third century as one of the world's great universities."

In addition to borrowing the Block M from the Athletic Department, the university has aligned its mission with the fight song. Speaking during the 2024 commencement ceremonies at the football stadium, Provost Laurie McCauley observed that a phrase from the song has "come to define our university. Drawing their power in part from what John Philip Sousa called the best college march ever written, the words have become an aspiration, a promise, and a daring credo: 'Leaders and Best.'"

Like the university at large, the Athletic Department is highly ranked. As of 2023, Michigan was one of only six programs nationally that had appeared in the top ten Directors' Cup rankings more than twenty times. The ranking is based on the success of colleges and universities in NCAA championships.

The Influential Day Report

Founding Michigan Ross dean Edmund Day played a key role in shaping athletics at Michigan. According to a Bentley Historical Library article ("The Michigan Stadium Story"), in the 1920s, the Michigan football stadium, Ferry Field, did not have enough seats to accommodate fans. The Athletic Department used a lottery system in which they mixed ticket applications in a clothes dryer, and local officials drew the winning applications.

In 1924, when Michigan Ross was founded, Athletic Director Fielding Yost proposed the construction of a new stadium under his "Athletics for All" plan. The University Senate decided that a committee should first investigate the athletic program. Dean Day headed the committee, and its report became known as the "Day Report." The Bentley Library article concludes that this was "probably the most significant single document in the development of Michigan's modern athletic program."

The report serves as a window into athletics in the mid-1920s. It opens by noting the place of physical education in the university, emphasizing that physical education is not an end in itself but is "a phase of general education. Bodily development has significance and value primarily as it is associated with corresponding growth of mind and character. In so far as physical health and strength, and accompanying habits of physical exercise and exertion, make possible a fuller realization of other capacities—be they mental, moral, or spiritual—the development of a sound and disciplined body becomes an integral part of any comprehensive educational program."

The report noted two spheres of physical activity at the university. The first, covering required physical education and intramural sports, affected all students.

The second, intercollegiate sports, was akin to an honors program that any student might join. "The Varsity squad constitutes the 'honors group.' . . . There is substantial good to be had from the general desire among the students to work up in any line of physical education or intramural sport until they can make the 'Varsity.' Under a properly constituted system, intercollegiate athletics should serve as an effective energizer of the general program of physical education at the University. In the opinion of the Committee it would be unfortunate if intercollegiate athletics on a fairly large scale were not maintained for this purpose."

The report summarized the benefits of intercollegiate athletics to the university. "[T]hey engender and give play to certain enthusiasms and loyalties which are valuable to alumni and students, and serviceable to the University. Intercollegiate contests are among the few occasions at which the entire student body comes together. The sense of common interest which animates the crowd at a football game plays a part in the development of common loyalties. . . . [I]t may well be argued that the association and concerted action developed among alumni and students in connection with intercollegiate athletics actually break the way for the development of association and concerted action on behalf of other and more important University projects."

11. Michigan Ross Ties to Athletics

The committee also recognized a danger associated with intercollegiate athletics. "The danger lies in the appearance of a kind of college spirit that is little more than vociferous support of athletic teams. . . . One of the most serious difficulties in intercollegiate football at the present time is the insistence of the alumni upon *winning* teams." [Emphasis in original.]

One section of the report highlighted "Some Evils of Intercollegiate Sports." It cited football as an example where "some of these evils are just now particularly serious." An evil that "seems to be at its worst in football is the pre-eminence of the coach. Football teams are referred to as if they were the personal possession of the head of the coaching staff."

Publicity of football stars was also thought to be excessive, the report noting that "If there is any sport in which the individual should be rarely singled out for praise it is in football, for in no other sport does success depend so completely upon the coordinated effort of all members of the team; yet the spotlight of newspaper publicity is commonly centered on the man who makes the pass or received it, or the man who happens to carry the ball in some open play. The inevitable result appears in the almost irresistible temptation offered football stars to join professional teams at extraordinary salaries."

Football coach Bo Schembechler echoed this concern over a half-century later in a legendary 1983 speech to the football team: "No man is more important than The Team. No coach is more important than The Team. The Team, The Team, The Team. . . . Because you can go into professional football, you can go anywhere you want to play after you leave here. You will never play for a Team again. You'll play for a contract. You'll play for this. You'll play for that. You'll play for everything except the team, and think what a great thing it is to be a part of something that is The Team."

The report concluded that intercollegiate athletics had grown out of proportion to other athletic and scholarly interests. The committee did recommend the construction of a new stadium, but one with "the utmost simplicity. No attempt should be made to give it the form of a monument or memorial." The report also proposed plans for developing intramural athletics and physical education, including the addition of athletic fields, swimming pools, tennis courts, a golf course, a gymnasium, and a fieldhouse for women.

One point of disagreement with Athletic Director Yost was the size of the new stadium. The report suggested seating 70,000–75,000, while Yost wanted 125,000–150,000. The Regents opted for the smaller size but also accepted Yost's proposal that the footings should be constructed to enable future expansion to accommodate over 100,000 seats. This compromise enabled later expansion, resulting in an attendance record of 115,109. Thus, the "Big House" became the largest stadium in the US and the third largest globally.

Student-Athletes

The Day Report noted two categories of student physical activities. In one category were regular students (called "Athletic Students" in the next section) who use the state-of-the-art physical facilities available on campus today. Students in the other category (the so-called "honors group") are varsity athletes, known today as student-athletes. Both categories are represented at Michigan Ross.

On April 28, 2024, I watched two Michigan Ross student-athletes in the second category during a dramatic victory over arch-rival Ohio State in the women's tennis Big Ten Tournament Championship at the Varsity Tennis Center. Michigan was ahead 3-2, and all but two matches had finished. Hundreds of fans watched the final two matches, knowing that Michigan needed to win one to secure the championship. If Ohio State won both, the Buckeyes would win.

The final two players were Michigan Ross students Kari Miller (ranked No. 3 nationally) at first singles and Julia Fliegner (ranked No. 27 nationally) at third singles. Julie fell behind in both sets before rallying to win, giving Michigan the championship and making it unnecessary for Kari to finish her match.

11. Michigan Ross Ties to Athletics

Both players were outstanding students. They were among the 139 Michigan student-athletes named Big Ten Distinguished Scholars in recognition of their grade-point averages of 3.7 or higher. Kari was also a first-team Academic All-America and, with Blake Corum (football), was named the 2023–24 Michigan Athlete of the Year.

When asked what she enjoyed about combining athletics with a business education, Kari observed, "What I have enjoyed most about being in the business school and being an athlete is both the academic and athletic rigor. Being part of strong programs both on and off the field has greatly helped me grow as a person."

Julia described her Michigan experience as "truly the perfect mix of academic and athletic excellence. . . . We've been incredibly successful this year as a team, and I wouldn't trade that for anything while I get an amazing undergraduate BBA degree."

Kari and Julia are among a long line of Michigan Ross students who excelled as varsity athletes. Many of these students played varsity sports while enrolled as undergraduate or graduate students, while others entered the graduate program after participating as undergraduates.

Some Michigan Ross athletes continue competing after graduation. For instance, Michigan was one of five universities that sent over forty scholar-athletes to the 2024 Paris Olympics. Four of these athletes were current or former Michigan Ross students.

Ron Johnson and Red Berenson are two notable examples of business school scholar-athletes who had outstanding professional careers.

Ron Johnson. Ron Johnson played varsity football while in the BBA program. During the three years (1966–68) he played for the Wolverines before graduating in 1969, he won the Big Ten Conference Medal of Honor (for his success in scholarship and athletics) and the business school's Leadership Award. Among his other honors:

- Big Ten Most Valuable Player
- First Team All-American
- NCAA Record for Most Rushing Yards in a Game
- Michigan Record for Career Rushing Yards

Following graduation, Ron played professional football for seven seasons and was the first New York Giants player to gain 1,000 yards in a season. He later became CEO of Rackson Corp., a food service company based in New Jersey.

Red Berenson. Gordon "Red" Berenson's career is especially notable because, after playing varsity hockey while enrolled in the BBA program, he played professional hockey, graduated from the MBA program, and returned to Michigan, where he was a highly successful hockey coach.

Figure 11.2. Red Berenson

11. Michigan Ross Ties to Athletics

Red grew up on the plains of Regina, Saskatchewan, where he was obsessed with playing hockey. A turning point in his life was when his father explained to him that lifetime salaries were much higher for people who graduated from college. This conversation led Red to think about life after his hockey career. He visited a local library to research the best universities with great hockey programs and quickly settled on the University of Michigan.

An All-American at Michigan, Red led the NCAA in scoring his senior year in 1962. The day after his final game at Michigan in 1962, he used his business education to negotiate his first professional contract (without using an agent) with the Montreal Canadiens. He played his first professional game that evening. He was the first player to move directly from a college career to the National Hockey League.

In those days, salaries were low, and players often had to take other jobs to supplement their income. But purchasing power was high. Red once told me that, although his initial salary was $7,000, he was able to purchase a four-bedroom house for $14,000.

In 1965, Red enrolled in the Ross MBA program. That year, the Canadiens won the Stanley Cup. He traveled to Ann Arbor to begin classes the day after the championship parade.

Red continued to play hockey while completing his MBA degree. One highlight of his seventeen-year professional career was setting a modern-day record by scoring six goals in a game. Later, he was named NHL Coach of the Year when coaching the St. Louis Blues.

In 1984, Red returned to Michigan as head coach. During his thirty-three years as coach, the Wolverines won two national titles, reached the Frozen (Final) Four eleven times, and qualified for the NCAA tournament a record twenty-two consecutive seasons. He is the fourth winningest coach in college ice hockey history.

Beyond his incredible coaching record, Red is known as a teacher who constantly reminded his players to focus on their studies and think about life after hockey. His former players have been successful as business leaders and in various other professions. As Dr. Chris Fox put it in a video called *Michigan Man: The Red Berenson Story*, "If I hadn't played hockey at Michigan, I wouldn't be a neurosurgeon." Dr. Fox played professional hockey before joining the Mayo Clinic. He was able to pay back the lessons learned from Red when he was on a medical team that helped Red's son recover from a closed head injury.

The Right Stuff. The skills necessary for success in sports and business are similar. As an article in *Dividend* (Spring 2005) put it, "The right stuff in sports is a lot like the right stuff in business."

Warde Manuel, one of my MBA students who was a two-sport athlete at Michigan and now serves as Michigan's athletic director, put it this way: "Many of the principles that guide us in athletics—in terms of teamwork, in terms of execution, in terms of how you model performance—are the same things that good businesses and good leaders use every day."

BBA Kalel Mullings was a member of the team that won the 2023 College Football National Championship, and in 2024 he had a sixty-three-yard run that coach Sherrone Moore called "one of the greatest runs in Michigan history." According to Mullings: "Football and business are actually very similar; it's just that one is a physical application, and one is a mental application. Both involve figuring out the best way to communicate and working in cohesion to achieve our goals."

Time management is an essential crossover skill between athletics and business. BBA graduate Jourdan Lawlor, a women's rowing team member, described one of her days: "Today I started at 5:30 and I have a midnight deadline for a business statistics group project. I'll probably be up until then finishing it. . . . You just try to squeeze everything in as much as possible while still trying to get six hours of sleep every night."

11. Michigan Ross Ties to Athletics

Michigan Ross student-athletes have found that their business education benefits them in various ways. Ron Johnson described negotiating his first contract with a professional football team: "We just couldn't come to terms. . . . I don't know whether the team thought I was bluffing or not, but I told my agent to tell them I might just go right on to graduate school and not play professional football at all. I was honestly willing to do that, and it's all because of my experience at the business school. I cannot tell you the strength that experience gave me in living my life."

Red Berenson recalled how his business school experience helped him as an athlete and coach: "I've always felt that going to the business school helped me as an athlete. . . . I thought I was a step ahead in my financial decision making and investments because of my experience in the business school. Then, as a coach, I don't think there's any question that running a team feels like running a business—although a not-for-profit—in terms of our public relations, our marketing, where we're spending our money, where we can generate more money."

One of my MBA students, Jeff Benz, was a member of the US Figure Skating Team and later headed legal affairs for the US Olympic Committee. He noted that skating is an individual sport, and he "wanted to benefit from the teamwork approach to problem solving that the Ross School of Business offers."

An article on several students who participated in varsity athletics while enrolled in Michigan Ross BBA or graduate programs highlighted other benefits from their business school education. According to gymnast Sierra Brooks (BBA '23): "I honestly find myself applying a lot of business concepts to my daily life, especially surrounding athletics. From how our team markets itself through social media or other channels, to thinking about the logistical and financial challenges our athletic department has to overcome every year. A lot of topics we covered in our management and organizations and business communications classes have affected how I think about leadership. I am constantly thinking about the unique communication styles we all have and the best strategies for getting teams to work well with one another."

Other benefits of their business school education cited by the Michigan Ross scholar-athletes include:

- "Working in diverse teams in the Ross classroom has taught me to be a more understanding, empathetic leader on my team." Annabelle Burke (BBA '24, Lacrosse)

- "I think the no-nonsense, problem-solving attitude of Ross has helped me in athletics and in school." Matt Frey (Master of Supply Chain Management '22, Baseball)

- "Most classes at Ross have curriculums that revolve around action-based learning, so I spent a lot of my time outside of the classroom working closely with classmates." Jess Speight (Master of Management '22, Football)

While business education benefits athletes, their athletic experience is also helpful in business. One of my former MBA students, Barry Klein, was a member of the US Olympic rowing team. He expressed appreciation for the discipline he learned from rowing: "Being disciplined to stay on a schedule, to do something every single day so you're working through not only the fun times but the low times and the mundane times, taught me a work ethic."

Mark Sorensen, an MBA student who played hockey for Michigan, feels that coping with adversity is the most important lesson from sports. "Having dealt with that through sports has really enabled me to strengthen my adversarial skills when it comes to business. You can't give up just because the mountain appears to be too high."

Another former hockey player, BBA graduate Strauss Mann, received the UM Carl Isaacson Award for combining high academic achievement with athletic ability. The lesson he learned from hockey is sound advice for any student: "A big part of my position is managing nerves, and going into a game very loose and trying to stay as present as possible so that I can just react in the moment while trusting my training. I've actually found that it's helped me a lot in taking tests and exams at Ross, just going in and letting go of the nerves inside so that in the exam I can be as efficient and logical as possible. I think sometimes people can get so nervous and start overthinking things that you can't just focus on the question and can't just focus on the puck and reacting to it."

Athletic Students

A recent survey asked Michigan Ross graduates, "What do you miss most about Ann Arbor?" Their responses ranked restaurant and food options #3, ahead of nightlife. As one alum put it, "The choices regarding food in Ann Arbor are world-class." Chapter 10 provides an example—Casa Dominick's, a popular restaurant located a few steps from the business school.

The graduates' top two choices relate to enjoying physical activity as a spectator or participant. The Michigan Wolverines topped the list. A special experience is joining 110,000 fans in cheering the football team on beautiful fall afternoons in the Big House, the largest stadium in the Western Hemisphere.

Outdoor activities ranked #2, which is not surprising given the area's over 150 nature areas and parks, a cross-county, border-to-border bike trail, and the university's two world-class golf courses. The courses were designed by Alister MacKenzie, who developed the Augusta National course that hosts the Masters Tournament, and Pete Dye, who planned TPC Sawgrass, home of The Players Championship.

In addition to the two golf courses, the university offers students several recreation buildings and an abundance of athletic experiences. These include:

III. Beyond the Michigan Ross Campus

- Leadership and Team-Building Adventure Trips
- Fitness Classes (ranging from slow-flow yoga to total body strength, including working with a personal trainer)
- Competitive Sports (including club sports that compete for national championships)

With its large esports program, competitive opportunities extend beyond physical activity at Michigan. In 2024, for example, the Michigan Esports Counter-Strike 2 team won the national championship. Like the football team, the esports team had a perfect season, including victories over Ohio State and Michigan State. Among the team leaders were Arcranic, nowalk, and ewege.

Ross Clubs: Dave Brophy and the Ice Hockey Club. Michigan Ross students also have many competitive opportunities within the business school, where clubs focus on ice hockey, skiing and snowboarding, outdoor pursuits, pickleball, and yoga. A Sports Business Association (SBA) also provides students with "opportunities to build and/or expand their network in the industry, learn from experienced professionals, understand the different functions and career paths, [and] develop a career plan." Participating companies in the annual SBA Sports Tech Conference in 2024 included the NBA, ESPN, NBC Sports, and the NFL Network.

Occasionally, faculty members become involved with Ross clubs. A notable example is finance professor Dave Brophy's enthusiastic support of the Ice Hockey Club. Dave, a native of Nova Scotia, had a remarkable professional career and personal life. He began teaching at Michigan in 1966 and retired in 2021—a record fifty-five-year teaching career.

Dave is a leading authority on venture capital and private equity investment. In 1980, he created the Michigan Growth Capital Symposium, the first university-based forum that brought together

11. Michigan Ross Ties to Athletics

investors and companies seeking funding. Based on the model he created, the US Securities and Exchange Commission issued a statement encouraging similar symposia around the country. Dave received many awards for his pioneering efforts, including the Lifetime Achievement Award from the Michigan Venture Capital Association.

On the personal side, Dave occasionally plays harmonica with the ten-member Mogue Doyle band, including at an annual Christmas event at an Ann Arbor Irish pub, Conor O'Neill's. The band has produced three albums and includes several of Dave's and his wife Linda's nine children: sons Greg, Mike, John, Tom, and David, and daughter Kathleen, the band's vocalist. The band is named after Dave's great-great-grandfather, Mogue Doyle, who led the Irish uprising of 1798 before emigrating to North America.

Apart from music, Dave's other personal passion is athletics. He played semi-professional baseball in Canada, ice hockey for Ohio State, and catcher on a business school team that won the city fastpitch softball championship. (Famed Michigan Ross marketing professor Tom Kinnear was the pitcher.)

In 1993, Dave was one of the founders of the Ice Hockey Club at Michigan Ross, comprised mainly of MBA students and alumni. His support included fund-raising that helped the players cover travel costs for tournaments where they played against MBA teams from Harvard, Dartmouth, Wharton, etc. He describes the experience as "good hockey and great socializing."

Dave also helped form a Michigan Ross women's team that played in tournaments. Four of his daughters—Ann, Kathleen, Colleen, and Amy—played for the team. He strongly advocates creating a varsity women's hockey team at Michigan and hopes his twin granddaughters, currently age three, can play for the Wolverines someday.

III. BEYOND THE MICHIGAN ROSS CAMPUS

Michigan Ross Faculty Interest in Intercollegiate Athletics

Beyond an interest in athletics within Ross, such as Dave Brophy's support of the ice hockey club, many business school faculty members are enthusiastic about intercollegiate athletics. Someone once asked me, "What do faculty talk about in the faculty lounge? Are there high-level discussions about research?" I had to admit that two topics dominate lounge conversations. While a visiting professor at Stanford, I discovered that the most animated discussions were about lack of parking. At Michigan, discussions often focused on athletics, particularly coaching errors in recent games.

Faculty interest in intercollegiate athletics falls into three camps. First, there are faculty members who participated in varsity athletics while students. Second, many faculty members have a general interest in varsity athletics, recognizing the value that sports add to the college experience at Michigan. Third, faculty members are directly involved with varsity and professional athletes in and outside the classroom.

Former Intercollegiate Athletes. Several business school faculty members were in the first camp—participants in varsity athletics. For example, finance professor Doug Hayes was on a mile relay team that set a Big Ten record that stood for fifteen years. Operations professor Roger Johnson represented New Zealand as a hurdler in the 1968 and 1972 Olympic Games. Captain of the UCLA track team, he set a New Zealand 400-meter hurdle record that stood for forty-two years.

Lindsay Gallo, my former BBA student and currently an accounting professor at Michigan Ross, is unusual in that she competed professionally for several years before earning her PhD in accounting. Lindsay was an All-American and NCAA champion in track while a Michigan undergraduate. Named the Big Ten Indoor Athlete of the Year, she was also Michigan's Big Ten Medal of

11. Michigan Ross Ties to Athletics

Honor winner for her athletic and academic success.

In an interview, Lindsay described the perspective she brings to the classroom as a former Michigan Ross student. She noted that undergrads don't necessarily appreciate "the type of research being done here and the resources available to you as a faculty member. The university has such a great support system for its faculty, which is not surprising since they have a great support system for its students and athletes. . . . Having been a student here, I know what they're going through. It gives me unique perspective. I'm excited to be on the other side of it, and hopefully, my experience as a student here will make me a more effective educator."

Faculty's General Interest in Athletics. In the second camp are faculty members who recognize the value athletics add to the college experience at Michigan. Michigan Ross faculty interest in athletics goes back to the beginning of the school. As noted in Chapter 1, founding dean Edmund Day attended a football game during a visit to Ann Arbor on November 9, 1922, before his appointment officially began. He wrote that he could "think of no better way to top off my visit than by witnessing a first-class gridiron contest." He later chaired the committee that prepared the "Day Report" described earlier in this chapter, perhaps the most influential document in the history of athletics at Michigan.

The correspondence of Paul McCracken, profiled in Chapter 6, illustrates faculty interest in athletics. Letters to and from Paul are peppered with references to athletics. Here are some examples:

- On October 18, 1974, President Gerald Ford wrote: "I understand that your sojourn in Washington was correctly timed to enable you to get back to Ann Arbor for the Michigan-Michigan State game. I wish I could have joined you."

- On August 26, 1996, Michigan athletic director Joe Roberson invited Paul to serve as a member of "an unofficial group of

III. Beyond the Michigan Ross Campus

senior experienced faculty members with whom I could informally discuss matters of athletic-academic relationships."

- September 10, 1997, a thank you to Joe Roberson for serving as athletic director.

- January 22, 1982, letter from former Michigan Ross student Edward Jennings after he had been appointed president of Ohio State University: "By the way, I will continue to root for Michigan . . . when appropriate!"

- February 21, 1984, letter to athletic director Don Canham thanking him for a "fascinating discussion last night. . . . I can see why you are generally deemed to be the premier athletic director in the American scene. On one of these occasions when a little daylight appears in the schedule, I may give you a ring just to see if you are free for lunch."

- February 23, 1984, thank you from Don Canham: "Your nice note brightened my day! I get so many letters from nuts that when someone intelligent writes me I think it's all worthwhile."

- April 7, 2000, to Bill Martin, expressing appreciation for accepting the athletic director position.

Why did Paul remain at Michigan Ross when he could have taught anywhere? In an interview, he cited three reasons: "I found the faculty congenial, my family liked it here, we had a good football team."

Faculty comments about athletics are not limited to internal communications. Feisty accounting professor Bill Paton (profiled in Chapter 5) expressed his feelings about a *Detroit Free Press* reporter in a letter to the editor dated October 19, 1949: "In recent weeks, with Michigan's football losses to Army and Northwestern as an

11. Michigan Ross Ties to Athletics

excuse, this chap Devine has let loose a barrage of gloating, abuse, and misrepresentation that goes beyond anything I have ever seen before appearing under the cloak of news reporting." Bill suggested that "brother Devine and his ilk should be fired or gagged."

Faculty Direct Involvement with Athletics. The third camp covers faculty members directly involved with athletics at the varsity or professional level. The Champions for Life program provides an example. During the 2016–17 academic year, Michigan Ross professors Kim Cameron and David Mayer conducted workshops on embracing change, developing team culture, and team-building for varsity basketball players and coaches. The basketball team won that year's Big Ten tournament championship and played in the national championship game the following year.

Faculty involvement with professional athletes is illustrated by a Michigan Ross partnership with the NFL to develop workshops for players. In 2015, for instance, faculty member Francine Lafontaine led a workshop on franchising for current players and retired veterans like Drew Brees. The following year, the NFL and the business school launched an expanded program called the NFL Business Academy that included management, entrepreneurship, franchising, and real estate. In conjunction with the program, faculty co-director Len Middleton led a webinar on how to evaluate business ideas and plan to start a business.

Michigan Ross also offered an educational program for athletic directors and others working in athletic departments nationwide. Called the Sports Management Institute, the program covered marketing, financial decision making, leadership, communications, legal issues, and negotiation (which I taught).

Personal Memories

While recognizing that every faculty experience with athletics is different, I offer mine as an example. My interest in athletics originated as a participant. Despite a slow start (my father cut me from his Little League team), I played varsity football and tennis in college. This unusual combination was possible at a Division 3 college (the College of Wooster). On arrival at Michigan in 1967, I played on the Law School tennis team that won the graduate championship. I also joined the Boxing Club, although an uppercut to the head by someone smaller than me was a wake-up call that caused me to abbreviate that experience.

As a Michigan graduate student no longer participating in varsity athletics, I had the opportunity to watch games as a spectator for the first time when UM played Duke in 1967. (Later, after joining the faculty, I felt at home in the Michigan stadium when I heard the voice of announcer Howie King. Howie had recently moved to Ann Arbor from Wooster, where he had announced the games in which I played.)

Enthusiasm for the team that year was low. After an opening victory, the team lost five straight games and finished 4-6. The stadium was little more than half-full during the final game against Ohio State. My college friend Jon Marti and I watched from the end zone, surrounded by empty seats. This made it easy to retrieve footballs following extra-point attempts.

My enthusiasm as a spectator changed dramatically when Ohio State next visited the stadium two years later. Top-ranked and defending national champion, OSU had one of the best teams in college history—a team that, some felt, could beat pro teams. In one of the greatest upsets in history, Michigan won the game 24-12 and started the "Ten-Year War" between Ohio State coach Woody Hayes and Michigan coach Bo Schembechler. As MBA graduate Stephen Sanger, former CEO of General Mills, put it: "After Bo's first season, anyone who attended the 1969 Michigan-Ohio State game dates Michigan football from that point."

With this background interest in athletics, I began interacting with athletics in class and through recruiting when I returned to

11. Michigan Ross Ties to Athletics

campus as a faculty member in 1974.

Athletes in Class. The most apparent form of faculty interaction is with athletes in the classroom. Here is a sampling of athletes who have taken my business law and real estate law courses. They were all serious students as well as outstanding athletes.

Bubba Paris. Bubba was an All-American tackle who later played several years for the San Francisco 49ers. He was large by 1980s standards, and I had difficulty seeing the student sitting behind him when Bubba sat at the front of the class.

Bubba once told me about his poor childhood in Louisville and how a severe injury during his first year at Michigan changed his life. Before the injury, his life centered on football. The injury caused Bubba to realize that his playing career might be limited, and he began to focus on his studies, eventually becoming a second-team Academic All-American. He currently serves as the executive director of a West Coast foundation.

Rob Lytle. Rob was an All-American running back who set the Michigan career rushing record and was the Big Ten's Most Valuable Player. In one game against Michigan State, he carried the ball ten times and averaged eighteen yards a carry. He finished third in the 1976 Heisman Trophy voting. Following graduation, Rob joined the Denver Broncos and scored the only touchdown when the team played in the Super Bowl during his rookie season.

Rob told me he took my course on enterprise organization because his father and uncle owned a clothing store in Fremont, Ohio, and he wanted to learn how partnerships and corporations are organized. Following his professional football career, he returned to Fremont and joined the family business before becoming a bank vice president. He was also active in community service, including serving as an assistant coach at Fremont High School when Charles Woodson played for the team.

III. Beyond the Michigan Ross Campus

Paul Heuerman. Paul was captain of the basketball team and a second-team Academic All-American. Drafted in the fifth round by the Phoenix Suns in 1981, he eventually pursued a legal career and is a real estate lawyer in Naples, Florida.

When Paul applied to law school, he showed me a letter of recommendation from Indiana basketball coach Bobby Knight. Knight had a public image as a bully and a tyrant. When he passed away in 2023, a *Wall Street Journal* obituary (November 1, 2023) noted: "He was as volatile and violently intense as anyone in the sport, accused at various times in his career of punching colleagues, bullying subordinates and fans, head-butting players, hitting opposing coaches, assaulting a police officer and chucking a potted plant at a secretary."

The letter Paul showed me revealed a kinder, gentler version of Knight. Paul told me that an Indiana player lost his footing during a basketball game. He would have fallen on his back and sustained a serious injury had Paul not caught him. In doing so, Paul received a foul. In his three-page handwritten letter of recommendation, Knight described the incident and praised Paul for his high values.

Rob Pelinka. Rob played basketball for Michigan. Despite the rigors of practice and travel, he was named the NCAA Walter Byers Scholar Athlete of the Year during his senior year at the business school. He graduated *cum laude* from the Michigan Law School and became a sports agent, representing top players like Kobe Bryant, James Harden, and Kevin Durant. He is currently the General Manager of the Los Angeles Lakers.

Rob played on three Final Four basketball teams at Michigan. During his last Final Four game, North Carolina led Michigan by two points with seconds remaining. Michigan's Chris Webber, trapped in a corner, called a timeout, which resulted in a technical foul because Michigan had no timeouts left. North Carolina took possession and won the game. Rob once told me that the night

11. Michigan Ross Ties to Athletics

before the game, he had a dream in which he was in that corner and shot a three-pointer to win the game.

Recruiting. My friend Don Nehlen was an assistant football coach at Michigan from 1977–79 before becoming the head coach at West Virginia University, where he set the record for most wins in the school's history. Don asked me to meet with recruits interested in business to explain the business school curriculum. After doing this for a few years, I also became involved with basketball and tennis recruiting.

The recruits would often bring family members with them. One of them, Justin Fargas, brought his father, Antonio, who starred in the TV show *Starsky and Hutch*. Justin played for Michigan before transferring to Southern California. He later played seven seasons for the Oakland Raiders. Charles Woodson brought his mother, Georgia, whom he later called "the greatest lady alive" during his remarks after winning the Heisman Trophy.

One famous father was a no-show. Michigan basketball coach Bill Frieder (a Michigan Ross BBA and MBA graduate) asked me to meet with an athlete he was especially interested in recruiting. He told me the athlete's father, Calvin Hill, played professional football. The day before the meeting, Bill called to tell me the meeting was canceled because the athlete, Grant Hill, had decided to attend Duke.

Although most of my meetings were at the business school, on Saturday, October 17, 1979, I met football recruit Milt Carthens at the Campus Inn for breakfast. The team spent the night before its home games at the hotel, and they were scheduled to play a homecoming game against Indiana that afternoon. After breakfast, the coaches took Milt to the players' rooms and invited me to join them.

At one of the rooms, the coaches had to knock loudly to wake the freshman player inside. When he finally opened the door, I was surprised to see how small he was, and I silently wondered whether the coaches had made a recruiting mistake. Later that day, Michigan was tied with Indiana with six seconds left and the ball on the Indiana forty-five-yard line. In what some consider the greatest play in Michigan history, quarterback John Wangler threw a touchdown pass to the freshman I had met that morning, Anthony Carter, to win the game.

Alumni

Athletic Directors. Of the twelve leaders who served as athletic directors since 1898, two are Michigan Ross MBA graduates. Bill Martin founded a large real estate development company before serving as Michigan's athletic director from 2000–2010. A world-class sailor, he represented the United States in the 1981 Admiral's Cup and later served as president of the US Olympic Committee. Bill refused to accept compensation for being athletic director, noting that "Michigan has been great to me. It is the least I can do for Michigan." He also donated over $1M to Michigan Ross.

Bill's competitive spirit, which led to his success in business and sports, was reflected in a quote posted on the door to his office: "Every morning in Africa, a gazelle wakes up. It knows it must outrun the fastest lion or it will be killed. Every morning in Africa a lion wakes up. It knows it must run faster than the slowest gazelle or it will starve. It doesn't matter whether you're a gazelle or a lion. When the sun comes up, you'd better be running."

Current athletic director Warde Manuel was a two-sport (football and track) athlete as an undergraduate at Michigan. Before accepting the athletic director position in 2016, he was the director of athletics at the University of Connecticut and SUNY Buffalo.

Warde entered the MBA program because "I wanted to learn the business principles that will help drive success in my career, and it's been an invaluable part of my education. In my understanding of how to lead, I learned how to manage, how to develop and invest the resources in a proper way to make us stronger and make us better as an athletic department."

11. Michigan Ross Ties to Athletics

In 2024, the College Hall of Fame and National Football Foundation named Warde the recipient of the prestigious John L. Toner Award in recognition of his administrative ability and dedication to college athletics. During the first seven years of his leadership, sixty-one Michigan athletes earned Academic All-American honors, and 535 were named Big Ten Distinguished Scholars. Warde has also served as president of the National Association of Collegiate Directors of Athletics.

Owners. Michigan Ross alumni have owned various professional sports teams. Steve Ross owns the Miami Dolphins and co-founded RSE Ventures, which created the International Champions Cup, a global soccer tournament. In addition to his gifts to the business school, Steve donated $100 million to athletics, which enabled the university to develop what is now called the Stephen M. Ross Athletic Campus. The campus includes state-of-the-art facilities that enable athletes to succeed in the classroom and on the field.

BBA graduate Bill Davidson was a member of the track team at Michigan and played Armed Forces football during World War II. He owned several sports teams, including the Detroit Pistons, Detroit Shock (Women's NBA), Detroit Fury (Arena Football League), Tampa Bay Lightning (National Hockey League), and Detroit Vipers (International National Hockey League). During one year, the Pistons won the NBA championship, the Lightning won the Stanley Cup, and the Shock won the WNBA championship.

Thanks to Bill, I attended my first professional basketball game. When I was associate dean, he invited Dean Joe White and me to watch the Pistons play the Golden State Warriors. Bill's limo took us to the Pistons' arena, the Palace of Auburn Hills, where we had dinner in a private dining room before heading to our seats at one end of the floor, a few feet from one of the baskets. Actors Jack Nicholson and Danny DeVito, who were in town to shoot the movie *Hoffa*, sat a few seats away from us.

III. BEYOND THE MICHIGAN ROSS CAMPUS

Well-Rounded Graduates

The Bentley Historical Library, where I researched this book, sits next to the presidential library honoring President Ford, whom I met when he spoke at Michigan Ross in 1978. One afternoon, during a break from my research, I wandered over to the Ford Library and discovered a special exhibit on "Gerald Ford: A Sporting Life."

President Ford was an outstanding scholar-athlete at Michigan. He played on two national championship football teams and was selected as the most valuable player on another team. Despite offers from the Green Bay Packers and Detroit Lions to play professional football, he decided to attend Yale Law School, where he graduated in 1941. His primary loyalty was to Michigan, where the Gerald R. Ford School is a leading public policy school. While president, Ford asked the White House band to play the Michigan fight song instead of "Hail to the Chief."

President Ford summarized his belief in the importance of competition in an article he wrote for *Sports Illustrated* (July 8, 1974): "Broadly speaking, outside of a national character and an educated society, there are few things more important to a country's growth and well-being than competitive athletics."

According to the library exhibit, Ford's participation in athletics shaped his belief in "the value of teamwork and the sense of fair play that became the hallmarks of his political career." Sports taught him "how to live, how to compete but always by the rules, how to be part of a team, how to win, how to lose and how to come back and try again."

At one time, the *Wall Street Journal* published rankings based on annual surveys of recruiters to find out what they looked for in business schools and their graduates. Michigan Ross and Dartmouth Tuck dominated these rankings. A *Journal* article that accompanied one of the surveys noted that "recruiters commend Michigan for its 'well-rounded' students who work competently in teams and possess

11. Michigan Ross Ties to Athletics

strong interpersonal skills."

Michigan is an ideal environment for well-rounded students. The article notes that the school's "practical focus resonates with corporate recruiters. . . . Now more than ever, companies are seeking M.B.A.s who are ready to roll their first day on the job." In the words of one recruiter, "Michigan students are prepared to function well in any position that they are given."

Michigan Ross students can complement these skills with the competition emphasized by President Ford. Some students, like Ford, are scholar-athletes. Other students use Michigan's world-class athletic facilities while participating in university programs and Michigan Ross clubs. Still others opt for competitive experiences that don't require physical activity, like the large esports program that produced a national champion in 2024. Combining their business school education with these competitive opportunities enables students to develop the well-rounded perspective valued by recruiters and important to success.

PART IV

THE SECRET SAUCE AT MICHIGAN ROSS

Chapter 12. The Secret Sauce at Michigan Ross

Chapter 12

The Secret Sauce at Michigan Ross

WHAT IS THE secret sauce that enabled the evolution of Michigan Ross from a school with twenty-two students in 1924 to a leading business school with a worldwide impact today? I began thinking about this question in 1995 when Dean Joe White asked me to head the school's strategic planning in addition to my responsibilities as associate dean for executive education.

The People of Michigan Ross

The strategic planning process included creating a Strategic Planning Committee, which identified the school's distinctive capabilities by examining stakeholder needs in light of environmental changes in management education. A key takeaway from this experience was that four categories of people are vital ingredients in the Michigan Ross secret sauce: students, faculty, staff, and alumni.

Students. From its initial enrollment of twenty-two students, the school has grown to over 4,000 students enrolled in the BBA program and various MBA and one-year master's programs. The best students in the world compete for positions in these programs. The average GMAT score of students starting the MBA program in 2023 was 719, and on average, they brought around six years of work experience to the program. In 2023, 9,210 applicants competed for 818 positions in the BBA program.

IV. The Secret Sauce at Michigan Ross

In addition to its degree program offerings, Michigan Ross is a leader in providing executive education to business leaders. In 2023, the *Financial Times* named the school the top executive education provider in North America. Participants in these programs have used their executive education experience to develop new processes that benefit their organizations.

Faculty. The achievements of Michigan Ross faculty can be summed up in one word: impact. Earlier chapters have provided numerous examples. Dean Edmund Day (Chapter 1) laid the foundation for a world-class business school. Bill Paton (Chapter 5) shaped the modern profession of accounting. Paul McCracken (Chapter 6) influenced US public policy through his advice to eight presidents over forty-eight years. Mary Bromage and Al Edwards (Chapters 7 and 8) were pioneers in enabling women and minority students to benefit from business education. CK Prahalad (Chapter 9) created concepts that shaped international business strategy and showed how businesses can achieve success while alleviating poverty. These are just a few of the hundreds of faculty members who, like beloved Doc Wolaver (Chapter 2), have developed students into leaders of organizations worldwide.

12. The Secret Sauce at Michigan Ross

Figure 12.1. Banner recognizing the Michigan Ross centennial

The theme of the Michigan Ross centennial in 2024 is "100 years of impact." As part of the centennial, the school's website provides one hundred examples of the faculty's impact on teaching and research. While in some cases this impact results from individual efforts, faculty members also collaborate to create entirely new fields of teaching and research. For example, faculty members Kim Cameron, Jane Dutton, and Bob Quinn founded the Center for Positive Organizations (CPO) to encourage research on how leaders can create positive work environments and enhance employee engagement. The Academy of Management has honored CPO for creating a new field in management and for "its extensive influence on management practices."

IV. THE SECRET SAUCE AT MICHIGAN ROSS

Faculty teaching and research have a ripple effect on management education through the school's PhD graduates. Chan Kim and Gary Hamel are among the graduates who have achieved international recognition for the impact of their ideas. As noted in Chapter 9, when CK Prahalad was named the outstanding management thinker in the world, they ranked in the top ten.

Faculty instruction is augmented by business leaders and other guest speakers at Michigan Ross—such as Malcolm Gladwell (author), Jalen Rose (retired professional athlete), Angela Davis (activist), Harry Belafonte (entertainer), and Andrew Young (politician)—who address challenges faced by business and society.

Staff. Staff members are the unsung heroes at Michigan Ross. They provide essential administrative and library support for faculty teaching and research. They decide which of the thousands of talented applicants are admitted to degree programs. They support students throughout their years at Michigan and help them launch careers.

Staff members handle the essential functions that are important in any organization, such as finance, HR, IT, marketing communications, and operations. They administer the renowned Executive Education Center and its Executive Residence. They provide various services to alumni, including scheduling events, creating networking opportunities, and developing career resources. They staff the centers, institutes, and initiatives that spark the innovation that characterizes Ross. They also provide opportunities for donors to match their interests with the school's needs.

Alumni. No stakeholders are more important to Michigan Ross than its alumni. As a school, we measure our success by their success. Alumni have been successful in a wide range of occupations, indicating that a Michigan Ross education, while oriented toward a business career, can serve as a gateway to many career opportunities. In the words of BBA graduate GS Suri: "The business school

12. The Secret Sauce at Michigan Ross

prepares you to sing, swim, fly, jump, hike, in any direction and to get to the top of the mountain at the end of the day. That's what I think is so cool about this place, because at med school, they teach you to be a doctor; at law school, they teach you to be a lawyer; at social work school, they teach you to be a social worker. At Michigan Ross, they teach you to be whatever you want to be in the world. I don't think there are a lot of institutions with that culture."

Here is a pop quiz that illustrates some possible career options. Which of the following UM alumni did *not* graduate from the business school?

1. Brad Keywell, co-founder of Groupon

2. David Connell, first executive producer of *Sesame Street*

3. John DeLorean, founder of the DeLorean Motor Company that produced the car used to travel through time in *Back to the Future*

4. Hal Sperlich, creator of the minivan

5. John Fahey, former CEO of the National Geographic Society

6. Terence Davis, former secretary general of the Council of Europe

7. Lynn Isenberg, producer and writer (*The Funeral Planner*, etc.)

8. Tusshar Kapoor, Bollywood actor

9. Dr. Paul Taheri, CEO of Yale Medicine and deputy dean of Yale School of Medicine

10. Richard Liu, news anchor for MSNBC and CNN

Answer: This is a trick question. They *all* graduated from the business school, where, as GS Suri noted, "they teach you to be whatever you want to be in the world."

Alumni During the Early Days. Alumni have been enthusiastic about Michigan Ross since the school's founding. On April 22, 1929, the first class (1926 graduates) announced to other alumni the May 11 date of what was to become an annual alumni conference.

The announcement recognized the importance of contact "between the alumni, the student body, and the faculty. The interests of the three groups are definitely connected and it is hoped that the conference plan will be of benefit to each. Possibilities for service between the groups will increase as the years go on and it seems highly desirable, therefore, that steps be taken now to make possible a closer contact between the alumni body and those who are more actively engaged in the work of the school." The conference schedule included interest group meetings, a luncheon talk by the dean, a Michigan-Illinois baseball game, and an evening banquet.

The following month, on May 7, 1929, Bert Wertman, class of 1928, sent a newsletter to his classmates, who learned that:

- Boots Kauffman's wife "presented him with an 8-1/2 pound boy."

- "Great Oaks" Brimmecombe "still has his moustache and smokes Chesterfields."

- Ken Church works in brokerage audits; he "falls short of being a real brokerage man, though, because he doesn't wear spats or a derby."

- Stan Ford "tells me he weighs over 160 pounds now."

- "Our noble president has purchased a radio for his family. . . . He said he heard Prof. Ross broadcasting from A2 the first

12. The Secret Sauce at Michigan Ross

night he had it, and almost thought himself back in Tappan Hall."

The Wall Street Crash, occurring later in 1929 and followed by the Great Depression, undoubtedly affected the alumni. A newsletter from Wertman, sent on December 15, 1931, listed classmates who had not paid their one-dollar dues and reported a cash balance of only $4.99.

Support by Alumni. The close contact between the school and alumni mentioned in the April 1929 letter has continued. The support provided by alumni has created the critical edge that differentiates a good school from a great one. The incredible naming gift of $100 million from Steve Ross in 2004, followed by his additional gifts of $150 million, enabled the school to complete a 179,000-square-foot campus and fund the most advanced technology, student scholarships, and signature action-based learning experiences.

The vital support other alumni provide is symbolized by a wall in the school covered with plaques honoring over seventy-five graduates who have each donated over $1 million to Michigan Ross. These gifts have funded physical facilities on the Michigan Ross campus, as well as institutes, centers, initiatives, programs, professorships, and scholarships that enable the school to retain its leadership position.

When students graduate, they join the world's most enthusiastic alumni community. Over 56,000 Michigan Ross alumni are part of a network of over 682,000 UM alumni from 179 countries. In the words of Michigan Ross graduate Kendall Verbeek, "It always surprises me how widespread the Michigan alumni network is. I wear clothing identifying me as a Michigan Ross alumna whenever I go somewhere new because it almost always results in interesting conversations and/or valuable connections." It is no surprise that alumni like to close their messages with "wherever you go, Go Blue."

IV. The Secret Sauce at Michigan Ross

"Go Blue" Humanity on Display. People affiliated with Michigan Ross—as students, faculty, staff, or alumni—are part of a lifelong community symbolized by the "Go Blue" fist pump. While most apparent at events like football games, the sense of community runs deep and emerges during day-to-day activities and in other circumstances.

Here is an example provided by my faculty colleague Jane Dutton, the Robert L. Kahn Distinguished University Professor Emerita of Business Administration and Psychology. A highly decorated scholar whose research has increased our understanding of fostering human flourishing at work, she is also an outstanding teacher and co-founder of the Center for Positive Organizations. In addition to her professional accomplishments, Jane is a humble person who shows compassion and concern for colleagues, family, and friends daily. The following facts are based on a case she authored with Monica Worline and Peter Frost titled "Three Students and a Fire."

Mid-February 2000 was an incredibly hectic time at the business school. Students prepared for half-term final exams, completed group projects with their teams, and met with corporate recruiters on campus. Faculty members wrapped up teaching assignments, graded end-of-term papers, and planned for the next half-term. Staff members supported faculty and students as they transitioned from one term to the next. In addition to his usual responsibilities, Dean Joe White prepared his most important talk of the year, the annual State of the School address to the entire school.

On February 15, at 3:00 a.m., a fire destroyed an apartment on Hill Street where three MBA students lived. Standing in their pajamas in the snow, the women watched as the fire consumed their belongings. What happened during the rest of the day demonstrates the power of the Go Blue spirit.

A faculty member driving to work noticed the fire and spotted one of her students. Within the next hour, she emailed a female faculty group called Neighbors asking for help, alerted the dean's

12. The Secret Sauce at Michigan Ross

office to the students' needs, and started a process that enabled the students to stay at the Executive Residence, the hotel on the Michigan Ross campus where executives stay when attending executive education programs. She also contacted the president of the Global Citizenship Club, a student organization devoted to community service.

After hearing about the fire, staff members immediately kicked into action. They arranged an interest-free $3,000 loan for each student and expedited the process for them to obtain IDs. They obtained laptops for the students. They finalized arrangements for the students to move into the Executive Residence. This flurry of activity reminded one staff member that "If there's one thing I've learned about this place, it thinks of itself as the best. People here think that they can do anything. It's like someone infused the place with the idea that nothing is impossible."

At a time when they faced exams, final assignments, and interviews, students dropped everything to help the women. The President of the Global Citizenship Club (GCC) emailed students asking for help and immediately received one hundred replies. She also created a donation box that students used to contribute $1,800 by the end of the day.

As often happens during crises, leadership emerged from unexpected places. In response to the GCC email, a student from South Africa volunteered to coordinate student efforts to help, such as working with over fifty students to replace the students' books, notes, and materials for their courses. He thought: "I'll just put up my hand in the air and tell people to come to me. You know, so they know who to ask about what needs to be done. Then I can coordinate and tell people what is left to be done, and we won't duplicate our efforts."

The day after the fire, one of the students who lost everything in the fire realized that she had no pencil or paper when she walked into class. At that point, a student approached her and gave her a new backpack filled with pencils, pens, pads of paper, computer disks, mints, a toothbrush, and a comb. Surprised, she said, "Thank you so much. I feel like you all are thinking of things before I even realize I need them." He responded, "Hey, what else are us cutthroat MBA types good for?"

Help also came from the alumni community. One alum heard about the fire from his son, who was in the same program as the students who lost their belongings. He sent a check for $5,000 to the dean, requesting to remain anonymous. He enclosed a note with the check: "As an alumni of the school, if there is anything I can do to help, I want to help."

Near the end of the day, Dean White gave his State of the School address as planned. Before beginning the talk, he left the podium, walked to the front edge of the stage, and recounted what had happened to the students and the community response. Looking back on the events a few days later, he observed: "If you ask me, the single most important thing that as leaders we can do is to make it fine, acceptable, and legitimate to put your humanity on display." If we do that, he noted, "it's unbelievable what you can unleash."

Beyond People

The importance of people as an essential ingredient in the secret sauce at Michigan Ross begs the question: What additional ingredients attract these high-quality individuals to Michigan Ross?

Although I had my own thoughts about this question, I asked ChatGPT for a second opinion by asking: "What is the secret sauce that made Michigan Ross a great business school?" The answer noted the importance of people (such as faculty who "are leaders in their fields" and a "robust and engaged alumni network") and included two additional ingredients that matched my conclusions. According to the AI analysis, these ingredients "combine to create a dynamic and supportive environment that prepares students for successful careers in business."

12. The Secret Sauce at Michigan Ross

An Action-Based Approach to Learning. One of these ingredients is the school's action-based approach to learning, where "students work on real business challenges for companies around the world." ChatGPT notes that this approach is complemented by an innovative curriculum, strong connections with leading companies that facilitate corporate projects, and a global perspective that enables international projects.

The action-based learning environment is difficult for other schools to imitate because it became embedded in the school's DNA when it was founded and has matured for a hundred years. The learning environment originated in the school's bylaws drafted by founding dean Edmund Day (Chapter 1) and approved by the Regents. The bylaws specified a curriculum enriched by research focusing on "the current problems of modern business" and cooperation with business concerns that is "necessary to the development of professional training."

Strong Sense of Community. The second ingredient mentioned by ChatGPT is a "strong sense of community and teamwork" fostered by "a collaborative environment where students work closely with peers from diverse backgrounds." The story of the fire earlier in this chapter illustrates this sense of community that unites students, faculty, staff, and alumni. As noted earlier in this chapter, one staff member said, "It's like someone infused the place with the idea that nothing is impossible."

Beyond the collaborative environment within the school mentioned by ChatGPT, a Michigan Ross education includes concern for the community at large. According to the bylaws drafted a century ago, this includes instruction "in the relationships between business leadership and the more general interests of the community, to the end that its students may be qualified as far as possible for positions of responsibility in business and for leadership in an industrial society."

IV. THE SECRET SAUCE AT MICHIGAN ROSS

As noted in the book *Tradition, Values & Change*, founding Dean Day "instilled in his students a concern for society and their effect upon it. This concept became part of the bedrock of the Michigan curriculum." In the words of the mission today, the school is positioned to "build a better world through business." Dean Sharon Matusik calls this mission the school's North Star.

Examples of Concern for Society. Various faculty, student, and staff activities illustrate the sense of community that translates into the school's bedrock concern for society. Students accept internships and are placed on boards of directors at nonprofit organizations. They take courses on sustainability, health delivery, urban entrepreneurship, socially-engaged design, and energy justice. Faculty share their research in these areas and brainstorm with students on how the research can have a positive impact. Action learning projects require the combined efforts of faculty, students, and staff. The result is a co-creation of knowledge, such as the bottom of the pyramid models that, in the words of CK Prahalad, show that "It's absolutely possible to do very well while doing good."

Michigan Ross alumni are especially well-positioned to impact society because of their success in leadership positions. Here are three examples of alumni who have had an impact on the Ross community and beyond.

Warren "Bud" Williamson. I first met Bud in 1996 after being named Williamson Family Professor of Business Administration. Bud and his brother JD graduated from Michigan Ross and have made major gifts to the school. Over the years, I enjoyed meeting with them in Ann Arbor and meeting members of their wonderful extended family when I was invited to give a talk at a family retreat in Stowe, Vermont, in 2011. I also have taught in a classroom named after JD.

Bud served as chairman of the board of WKBN Broadcasting Corp. and led the company's entry into the cellular telephone indus-

12. The Secret Sauce at Michigan Ross

try, where he served as chairman of Sygnet Wireless. While active in many community service organizations, Bud was especially passionate about creating what he called a "Geek Park."

My last meeting with Bud was at his home in Marco Island, Florida, in February 2022, when he was ninety-one. Although in ill health, he became animated when explaining that the park was the culmination of a long-held dream to create a place where students from kindergarten to college could work on science-related projects, such as drone research. Before Bud passed away the following October, he donated over two hundred acres to create what is today the Williamson Innovation Park.

David E. A. Carson. As noted earlier, staff members are the unsung heroes at Michigan Ross. Frank Wilhelme is a shining example. Frank was the second person hired when Dean Gil Whitaker created a new development and alumni relations program at Michigan Ross in 1980. Drawing on his ability to match the interests of alumni with the school's needs, Frank eventually moved into leadership positions, including serving as assistant dean for development, alumni relations, and major gifts during his thirty-year career at Ross. Over the years, he has also passionately supported the Bentley Historical Library.

In 2005, I met with Frank to discuss a new opportunity raised by Michigan Ross graduate David Carson. David was highly successful in Connecticut's insurance and banking industries. Before his retirement as CEO of People's Savings Bank, *Forbes* magazine named him one of the 500 "most powerful people" in corporate America.

Frank explained that David's influence extended beyond the business community. He served as an officer in several nonprofit organizations and testified before Congress on numerous occasions on business and social concerns. In recognition of his distinguished career, David has received four honorary degrees and the Ellis Island

IV. THE SECRET SAUCE AT MICHIGAN ROSS

Medal of Honor.

Based on his experiences on public policy matters, David felt that future business leaders should understand how government works to prepare them to develop effective strategies for participating in the public policy arena. Frank and I prepared a proposal to implement David's vision, resulting in the creation of the Carson Scholar Program. As program director for many years, I appreciated David's guidance and our close friendship that developed over the years.

Through this program, over 1,000 Ross BBA students have had the opportunity to learn about the public policy process during meetings with government and business leaders in Washington. A Dean's Office survey concluded that the program is the highest-impact learning experience in the BBA program. Here are examples of the program's impact, as reported by students:

- "The Carson Scholars Program is a powerful tool in understanding the interaction between business and government. The Program is as fundamental as finance and accounting to managing a business effectively. My experience at Bloomberg demonstrated one of the most important lessons of the Carson Scholars Program: that government decision-making is as integral as business decision-making to the speed and breadth of a company's operations and strategic development."

- "Businesses are greatly affected by the legal and policy frameworks in the nation and, as next generation's business leaders, it is our responsibility to shape policy for the betterment of society and businesses. The program cemented in me the importance of our government on business and I have since sought out further opportunities to become well-versed in politics to further my business career . . . [such as] at the White House in the Vice President's Communications Office."

12. The Secret Sauce at Michigan Ross

- "The Carson Scholar Program was nothing short of life-changing. It opened my eyes to new possibilities and ignited what was a spark of interest in government into a bonfire. I was so fascinated that I am now working on a PhD in Political Science where I am studying business regulation and economic development—kind of like getting a PhD in Carson Scholars curriculum!"

- "I use the information I learned, the network I built, and the skills I developed during the Carson Scholar program in my job and as an informed citizen of the US."

A similar opportunity was added to the Master of Accounting program as a result of a discussion I had with faculty colleague (and now associate dean) Cathy Shakespeare when she headed the program. Today, students begin their accounting studies with a symposium in Washington on how accounting policy shapes business.

Bill Davidson. One afternoon in September 1991, Dean Joe White asked me to stop by his office, where he described a lunch meeting he had just had with Michigan Ross graduate Bill Davidson. Joe told me that Bill was considering a significant gift to the school—in the neighborhood of $500,000. He showed me a sheet of paper, stained from the Chinese food they had enjoyed over lunch, where Bill had outlined his plans for a nonprofit institute.

Joe explained that creating the center might be complicated because Bill wanted the institute to be more independent than usual, which might require complex negotiations with the university administration and Bill's legal and tax staff. He asked me to work with Frank Wilhelme on these negotiations. Over the next several months, Frank and I trudged through the snow to the UM administration building and had numerous meetings with Bill's lawyers and tax experts before obtaining an agreement on a model that satisfied both sides. Frank noted it was "the most fascinating gift I

IV. THE SECRET SAUCE AT MICHIGAN ROSS

ever worked on."

While Frank completed the details, Joe and Bill agreed that the institute would focus on transition economics. On April 23, 1992, the school announced the creation of the William Davidson Institute (WDI) funded by Bill's gift of $30 million, at the time the largest gift to a US business school. Today, WDI is one of the world's leading centers devoted to emerging economies. Over 1,800 students have joined teams that have helped businesses and nonprofit organizations develop solutions to their problems.

During my fifteen years on the WDI Board of Directors, I appreciated the opportunity to observe Bill in action. Named by *The New York Times* as one of the most generous donors in America, he was a classic Michigan Ross graduate in his desire to have a positive impact on society. His business philosophy—"It can be done"—also applied to his actions in the social arena.

After Bill passed away on March 13, 2009, Dean Bob Dolan sent a message to the business school community. Referring to Bill as "Mr. D," Bob noted: "One of the great things in life is that you get to pick your teachers. Whom do you adopt as your model of behavior? Addressing a dilemma by asking, 'What would Mr. D do?' has always been a most worthwhile practice for me. It's a habit I plan on continuing, even though, sadly, my very enjoyable days learning from him have ended."

The community-oriented philosophy of these three alumni, and countless other graduates who have experienced a Michigan Ross education, was captured in a David Carson graduation speech that is reprinted in his biography, *Bow Tie Banker*: "It is not the achievement of material goals that will bring the days of great joy to your lives. No, the days of great joy come when your accomplishments are shared and sustained with business associates, the community where you live, your friends, and perhaps most importantly, with your families."

12. The Secret Sauce at Michigan Ross

The Michigan Ross Location. ChatGPT overlooked a final ingredient in the Michigan Ross secret sauce: its location within a world-class university in a unique college town, one of the best places to live in America. This location, combined with the other ingredients, attracts the high-quality people essential to the school's success.

As discussed in Chapters 10 and 11, faculty and students have abundant opportunities to study and conduct research in "top ten" programs throughout the university. In their off hours, they experience the cultural environment, dining experiences, and recreational opportunities that result in Ann Arbor's No. 1 ranking for quality of life. When asked how Michigan's culture differs from the two other large universities where he served as president, President Santa Ono replied that Michigan has an unusual esprit de corps, a spirit of loyalty and pride generated by the unique synergy between town and gown.

The 2124 Bicentennial

What will happen to Michigan Ross over the next hundred years? What will the school be like when celebrating its bicentennial in 2124?

Chapter 2 noted that on October 12, 1925, beloved professor Doc Wolaver opened his day pleased with the news that, as a result of the Locarno Treaty, Germany would never again declare war on other European countries. He had no clue that his youngest son would die as a teenager in Europe a few years later while serving in the infantry during World War II.

Doc, like others at the time, would have been unable to imagine that during the first hundred years of Michigan Ross history, the United States would deploy military forces overseas over 300 times, including during the Korean War, the Vietnam War, and the Gulf War. He would have been surprised to learn about advances in medicine, such as the development of antibiotics, vaccinations, and organ transplants. He would have been puzzled by technological developments that spawned a vocabulary that included words like Google, email, texting, computers, internet, iPhone, and artificial intelligence. He would have been saddened to learn about the assassination of a US president but pleased to hear about the fight for equal rights. He would have doubted stories about space exploration and the moon landing. Descriptions of natural and economic disasters like the Great Depression and a series of stock market crashes would have shocked him.

Like Doc Wolaver, it is difficult to imagine political, social, economic, medical, and technological developments between now and the celebration of the Michigan Ross bicentennial in 2124. Given the possibility that even death and taxes will become uncertain, the only certainty is that one hundred years from now, the world will radically differ from what it is today.

The secret sauce at Michigan Ross combines outstanding people, action-based learning, and a strong sense of community. These ingredients have been blended within a world-class university located in a vibrant city—and allowed to marinate for one hundred years. The result is a school with a tradition of excellence based on its powerful impact on business and society. As long as this secret sauce remains intact, Michigan Ross should be able to adapt to unknown future challenges and thrive as one of the world's great business schools.

Earlier chapters provide examples of the school's impact, such as the leadership of faculty members in shaping a profession, national policy, and global business strategy. This chapter describes how alumni like Bud Williamson, David Carson, and Bill Davidson used their business acumen to improve society. These examples represent the tip of the iceberg, as thousands of graduates in countries around the world continue to have a positive impact on society in their everyday lives. They, indeed, are the **Leaders and Best**.

From the Publisher

Thank You from the Publisher

Van Rye Publishing, LLC ("VRP") sincerely thanks you for your interest in and purchase of this book.

VRP hopes you will please consider taking a moment to help other readers like you by leaving a rating or review of this book at your favorite online book retailer. You can do so by visiting the book's product page and locating the button for leaving a rating or review.

Thank you!

Resources from the Publisher

Van Rye Publishing, LLC ("VRP") offers the following resources to readers and to writers.

For *readers* who enjoyed this book or found it useful, please consider receiving updates from VRP about new and discounted books like this one. You can do so by following VRP on Facebook (at www.facebook.com/vanryepub), Twitter (at www.twitter.com/vanryepub), or Instagram (at www.instagram.com/vanryepub).

For *writers* who enjoyed this book or found it useful, please consider having VRP edit, format, or fully publish your own book manuscript. You can find out more and submit your manuscript at VRP's website (at www.vanryepublishing.com).

Acknowledgments

I AM THANKFUL to many people who enabled me to engage in the labor of love represented by this book.

- I am grateful to my colleagues on the centennial team and to Francine Lafontaine for asking me to join the team.

- I express my appreciation to the Bentley Historical Library staff, who were incredibly knowledgeable and friendly. Even the Bentley custodian occasionally asked about my research and expressed concern about my standing over boxes of historical materials for hours on end. Caitlin Moriarty was especially helpful in promptly responding to my questions and suggesting how to proceed with the research. I also thank Corey Seeman, Director of Kresge Library Services at Michigan Ross, and Tara Start, Program Coordinator at the Paton Accounting Center, for their assistance.

- I want to extend my gratitude to the people of Michigan Ross—students, faculty, staff, and alumni—who are an essential ingredient in the secret sauce that has led to the school's success. I'd also like to thank President Santa Ono and Dean Sharon Matusik, who are leading the university and the school into the next hundred years.

- Special thanks to the individuals who have reviewed draft chapters of the book, including Dave Brophy, George

Acknowledgments

Cameron, Richard DeVarti, Jason Epstein, Tim Fort, Bill Hall, Nancy Hauptman, Herb Hildebrandt, Sidney Jones, Tom Kinnear, Vibhav Parikh, Deepa Prahalad, Cindy Schipani, Jim Walsh, Joe White, Frank Wilhelme, David Wooten, Brian Wu, and Stephen Zeff.

George Siedel
University of Michigan
Ann Arbor, Michigan

Notes

General Sources

General sources include the following. Chapter-specific sources are listed under each chapter heading.

Sources at the Bentley Historical Library:

1. Stephen M. Ross School of Business Records, 1916–2017

2. Stephen M. Ross School of Business Oral History Interviews, 1990–1992, 1999, 2005

3. School of Business Administration Publications, 1922–2017

4. University of Michigan History Subject Guide

5. *The Making of the University of Michigan: 1817–1992* by Howard H. Peckham

Other general sources:

1. The University of Michigan Millennium Project: http://milproj.dc.umich.edu

2. *Dividend* Historical Issues: https://www.bus.umich.edu/Kresgelibrary/resources/dividend/dividend.html

3. *Business Education at Michigan*: https://web.archive.org/web/20170630232207/https://michiganross.umich.edu/abo

Notes

ut/our-history/business-education-at-michigan-history

4. One Hundred Years of Impact: https://michiganross.umich.edu/about/100-years

5. *University of Michigan: An Encyclopedic Survey*: https://quod.lib.umich.edu/b/bicentennial/13950886.0010.001?view=text;rgn=main

6. *Tradition, Vision & Change*: https://drive.google.com/file/d/1iAgG6bZFRZlLUhGQeIaK1VnDW2VrdTcQ/view

7. *Always Leading, Forever Valiant: Stories of the University of Michigan*, Kim Clarke, ed., University of Michigan Press, 2017

Chapter 1. The Birth of Michigan Ross

In addition to the general sources listed previously, sources include:

1. Phelps, "The Early Days," *Dividend* (September 1986), on the first marketing course in the United States.

2. Information on the academic careers of students who took commerce courses offered by the Economics Department is from "What has Become of Some Recent Alumni of this School," published in *The Michigan Alumnus* (November 22, 1928).

3. Dean Day's nickname of "Rufus" is explained in a class note in the *Dartmouth Alumni Magazine*, November 1950, page 42.

4. The comment on how the thesis requirement "tried our souls" is from Phelps & Waterman. "Ann Arbor and the Business School in the Twenties," *Dividend* (Fall 1971).

Notes

5. Information on University of Michigan faculty members who became presidents of Cornell University is from "Cornell sustains presidential ties to University of Michigan," *Cornell Chronicle* (November 15, 2016).

Chapter 2. The Business School during the 1925–26 Academic Year

In addition to the general sources listed previously, sources include:

1. This interactive map was used to recreate Doc Wolaver's walk to the business school: http://specular.dmc.dc.umich.edu/map/drag/.

2. Doc's house is described at this site, which includes the quote about the "best food in Ann Arbor": https://aadl.org/buildings_hhaa049.

3. The account of the Loeb-Leopold case draws on "The Lives and Legends of Richard Loeb and Nathan Leopold," https://loebandleopold.wordpress.com, and "Leopold and Loeb's Criminal Minds," https://www.smithsonianmag.com/history/leopold-and-loebs-criminal-minds-996498/.

4. For a wonderful account of Professor White's tree-planting project, see "Professor White's Diag" by James Tobin: https://heritage.umich.edu/stories/professor-whites-diag/#:~:text=Two%20nurserymen%20from%20New%20York,State%20Street%20on%20the%20west. He tells the story of the Tappan Oak in "The Tappan Oak: A tale of life, death, and rebirth": https://michigantoday.umich.edu/2021/12/18/the-tappan-oak-a-tale-of-life-death-and-rebirth/.

5. The radio shows that Doc listened to in the evening are mentioned in "50 Years of Unique Radio": https://www.world

Notes

radiohistory.com/Archive-Station-Albums/WJR-50-Years.pdf.

6. Robert Frost's experience in Ann Arbor is recounted in "Robert Frost in Ann Arbor" by James Tobin: https://michigantoday.umich.edu/2010/06/09/a7771/.

7. Information on the business school's first female graduate, Sih Eu-yang Chen, is from the article "Early Women MNA Students Ushered in a New Era," *Dividend* (Fall 2006).

Chapter 3. The Business School at Age Fifty: The 1974–75 Academic Year

See the general sources listed previously.

Chapter 4. The Michigan Ross Centennial: The 2023–24 Academic Year

In addition to the general sources listed previously, sources include:

1. The podcast in which former dean Joe White describes the origins of MAP is at https://michiganross.umich.edu/news/episode-204-100-years-impact-ross.

2. Here is a link to the Negotiation Planner website: http://negotiationplanner.com.

3. Here is a link to the Coursera "Successful Negotiation" course: https://www.coursera.org/learn/negotiation-skills.

Notes

Chapter 5. William "Bill' Paton: Outstanding Educator of the Century

In addition to the general sources listed previously, sources include the William A. Paton papers, 1919–1984, at the Bentley Historical Library (the "Paton archive") and the following:

1. The comment about how Bill worked his way through college is from Herbert Taggart's contribution to "A Tribute to William A. Paton," *The Accounting Review* (January 1992).

2. The quote about dandelion greens, cabbages, and turnips is from Williams and Lawrence, *William A. Paton: A Study of His Accounting Thought* (Emerald Publishing, 2018).

3. The description of the meals Bill ate at the age of one hundred is from "Happy 100th," *Ann Arbor News* (July 15, 1989).

4. Kellogg's "cereal for dinner" campaign is described in "Shoppers call out Kellogg CEO's 'cereal for dinner' pitch for struggling families," *USA Today* (February 26, 2024).

5. The Pierpont quote is from "William A. Paton Dies at 101," *Dividend* (Spring 1991).

6. Bill's description of a memory game is from the Paton archive at the Bentley Historical Library.

7. The story about Bill giving a student a grade of C− is from Thomas Dyckman's contribution to the Paton tribute, *supra* note 1.

8. Bill's comment about reading 500 books yearly is from "Foe of pussyfooting turns 100," *The University Record* (July 3, 1989).

Notes

9. The quote on staying out of the middle of the road is from "A teacher affects eternity; he can never tell where his influence stops," *Dividend* (Fall 1989).

10. The quote about Bill being "red-headed, vigorous . . ." is from *Dividend*, *supra* note 5.

11. The quote about pussyfooting is from *The University Record*, *supra* note 8.

12. The quote about restoring public confidence is from Norton Bedford's contribution to the Paton tribute, *supra* note 1.

13. For a complete account of the Klein affair, see James Tobin's article "Lost Star": https://heritage.umich.edu/stories/lost-star/.

14. Bill's description of teaching during cross-examination is from the Paton archive at the Bentley Historical Library.

15. The Taggart quote on Bill's "dealing with students" is from *The University Record*, *supra* note 8.

16. The Townsend quote is from *Dividend*, *supra* note 5.

17. The Viravan quote and the quotes that follow it are from messages to Bill on his 100th birthday. They can be found in the Paton archive at the Bentley Historical Library. Some are also included in the *Dividend* article, *supra* note 9.

18. The quote about what Bill was most proud of is from the Williams and Lawrence book, *supra* note 2.

19. The "peer effect" is discussed in the book *The Peer Effect: How Your Peers Shape Who You Are and Who You Will Become* (2023) by sociologists Syed Ali and Margaret Chin.

Chapter 6. Paul McCracken: A Modest and Influential Advisor to Eight Presidents

In addition to the general sources listed previously, sources include the Paul Winston McCracken papers, 1943–2011, at the Bentley Historical Library and the following:

1. An article in *Ann Arbor Scene Magazine*: https://books.google.com/books/about/Ann_Arbor_Scene_Magazine.html?id=aO4MAQAAMAAJ.

2. Paul's memoir: https://apps.lib.umich.edu/faculty-memoir/apps.lib.umich.edu/faculty-memoir/faculty/paul-w-mccracken.html

3. An article on Paul's retirement in *Dividend* magazine (September 1986): https://apps.lib.umich.edu/faculty-memoir/apps.lib.umich.edu/faculty-memoir/faculty/paul-w-mccracken.html

Chapter 7. Mary Bromage: Navigating the Shoals of Discrimination

In addition to the general sources listed previously, sources include the Mary C. Bromage papers, 1862–1994, at the Bentley Historical Library and the following:

1. "It Was a Man's World" by Lara Zielin: https://bentley.umich.edu/news-events/magazine/it-was-a-mans-world/. This and the following sources were especially useful in researching the US Health, Education, and Welfare allegations in 1970.

2. "What Factors Led to the Success of the Historic 1970 Sex Discrimination Complaint Filed" by Sara Fitzgerald:

Notes

> https://search.alexanderstreet.com/view/work/bibliographic_entity%7Cweb_collection%7C2500262.

3. Professor Mary Maples Dunn's letter to President Fleming is at https://documents.alexanderstreet.com/d/1005577067.

Chapter 8. Al Edwards: A "Dean of Inspiration" Arrives After a Student Uprising

In addition to the general sources listed previously, sources include the following:

1. "An Integrated Life" by David Wooten, *Dividend* (Spring 2007).

2. Faculty Memorial: J. Frank Yates (1945–2020: https://lsa.umich.edu/psych/news-events/all-news/faculty-news/faculty-memorial---j--frank-yates--1945-2020-.html.

3. The closing quote is from the history of the Alfred L. Edwards Conference: https://ross.campusgroups.com/bbsaatross/ale47/#:~:text=Conference%20History,minorities%20in%20the%20business%20world.

Chapter 9. CK Prahalad: The World's Most Influential Thinker

In addition to the general sources listed previously, sources include a book of remembrances published by Michigan Ross titled *CK Prahalad: 1941–2010*. The book contains biographical information and comments from students, faculty, and the media quoted in this chapter. It includes sixty-one pages of media tributes alone. The chapter is also based on these sources:

Notes

1. CK's challenge to the University of Michigan is from "CK Prahalad Challenges Michigan to Expand World View," *Dividend* (Fall 2003).

2. CK's plan for India is from "Introduction: India@7," https://indiaat75.in/about-us/introduction/.

3. The Adi Ignatius quote is from "C.K. Prahalad," *Harvard Business Review* (April 17, 2010).

4. The information about the rejection of CK's paper by the *Strategic Management Journal* is from "C.K. Prahalad's Passions," by Wooten, Parmigiani, and Lahiri, *Journal of Management Inquiry* (June 2005).

5. CK's sheepdog metaphor is from "C.K. Prahalad: Top and Bottom of the Pyramid" by Des Dearlove: https://thinkers50.com/blog/c-k-prahalad-top-and-bottom-of-the-pyramid/.

6. The quotes from Professors Hart and London are from "Remembering CK Prahalad—Collected Thoughts," NextBillion: https://nextbillion.net/remembering-ck-prahalad-collected-thoughts/.

7. The Sachin Rao quote is from his article "Reflections on the MAP and Working with Dr. C.K. Prahalad," *Journal of Management Inquiry* (June 2005).

8. CK's story of the blind men and the elephant is from Dearlove, *supra* note 5.

9. The Archarya quote at the conclusion of the chapter is from "Today's Social Entrepreneur" by Nish Acharya: https://www.forbes.com/sites/nishacharya/2019/09/19/todays-social-entrepreneur-inspired-by-gandhi-taught-by-prahalad-leading-like-yunus/.

Notes

Chapter 10. The Best College Town and a Popular Student Hangout

In addition to the general sources listed previously, sources include the following:

1. For a discussion of Ann Arbor as a combination of Silicon Valley and Midwest values, visit the Ann Arbor Spark's website: https://annarborusa.org.

2. The quote on commuting from New York City to Ann Arbor is from "I commute every week . . ." (*Business Insider*, April 7, 2024).

3. President Obama's visit to Zingerman's is described on the deli's website: https://www.zingermansdeli.com.

4. The quotation about the poster-filled walls at Dominick's is from this article: https://punchdrink.com/articles/townies-and-students-unite-at-ann-arbors-everyman-bar/.

5. For additional information about the Ann Arbor Film Festival and its awards, visit https://www.aafilmfest.org.

6. The story about the creation of Oberon beer is from the Hopculture website: https://www.hopculture.com.

7. Information about the etched glass panels is from https://senate.michigan.gov/history/diduno.html.

8. To watch the *On Gallows Hill* trailer, visit https://www.indiegogo.com/projects/a-cult-classic-80s-horror-film-on-gallows-hill#/.

9. For information about the market capitalization of Dominos, visit https://companiesmarketcap.com/dominos-pizza/marketcap/.

Notes

Chapter 11. Michigan Ross Ties to Athletics Within a World-Renowned University

In addition to the general sources listed previously, sources include the following:

1. For the full text of President Kennedy's remarks, see "The Founding Moment": https://www.peacecorps.gov/about-the-agency/history/founding-moment/.

2. For additional information on the two statues at the Michigan Union, see "Exhibiting More Than Friendship and Character": https://annex.umma.umich.edu/post/156802683332/exhibiting-more-than-friendship-and-character.

3. The Hollinger essay on "Academic Culture at Michigan, 1938–1988" is available at https://www.rackham.umich.edu/downloads/Hollinger.pdf.

4. For the article on CEOs from Fortune 1000 companies and the Isom quote, visit https://michiganross.umich.edu/news/university-michigan-produces-more-ceos-fortune-1000-companies-any-other-public-university.

5. The Frost quotation about the football game is from "Frost and Burton at Michigan, 1921–26, Then and Now" by Paul Dimond: https://sites.lsa.umich.edu/mqr/2018/04/frost-and-burton-at-michigan-1921-26-then-and-now-by-paul-r-dimond/.

6. For information about branding the Block M, see https://alumni.umich.edu/michigan-alum/history-lessons-the-block-m-in-brief/.

7. "The Michigan Stadium Story" can be found at https://bentley.umich.edu/athdept/stadium/stadtext/stadbild.htm.

Notes

8. The Kari Miller quote is at https://michiganross.umich.edu/news/qa-hear-eight-michigan-ross-all-star-student-athletes-u-m-s-powerhouse-sports-teams-year.

9. The Julia Fliegner quote is at https://mgoblue.com/news/2024/4/10/womens-tennis-scholar-story-fliegner-blazes-new-path-of-business-art-history-and-law.

10. The information about Ron Johnson and the story about his professional contract is from "What Do Football, Hockey, and Bobsledding Have to Do with Executive Leadership?" *Dividend* (Spring 2005).

11. The information about Red Berenson is from "Michigan Man" (https://www.collegesportslive.com/video/mich/mens-ice-hockey/michigan-man-the-red-berenson-story-20220407181710629281/); "Scoring Goals on the Ice and in Life," *Dividend* (Fall 2017); and "Fire and Ice" (https://www.mlive.com/wolverines/2020/03/fire-and-ice-passion-for-game-still-burns-inside-michigan-hockey-legend-red-berenson.html).

12. The section on "The Right Stuff" is based on feature stories in "The Right Stuff in Sports and Business," *Dividend* (Spring 2005); "Four Michigan Ross Athletes Leading On the Field and in the Classroom" (https://michiganross.umich.edu/news/four-michigan-ross-athletes-leading-field-and-classroom); and "Hear From Eight Michigan Ross All-Star Student Athletes on U-M's Powerhouse Sports Teams this Year" (https://michiganross.umich.edu/news/qa-hear-eight-michigan-ross-all-star-student-athletes-u-m-s-powerhouse-sports-teams-year).

13. The Kalel Mullings quote is at https://michiganross.umich.edu/profiles/kalel-mullings.

Notes

14. The Strauss Mann quote is from featured alumni stories at https://michiganross.umich.edu/our-community/profiles.

15. For information on the survey of Ross graduates about what they miss about Ann Arbor, see https://www.youtube.com/watch?v=IdVMKQlBteA.

16. The Lindsay Gallo quote is from https://mgoblue.com/news/2014/8/27/Alumni_Spotlight_Dr_Lindsey_Gallo.

17. The McCracken quote about why he stayed at Michigan is from "Paul W. McCracken honored for 50 years of service to UMBS," *The Monroe Street Journal* (October 5, 1998).

18. The Sanger quote is from "General Mills former CEO to give $20 million to U-M," *Detroit Free Press* (January 14, 2015).

19. Information about Bill Martin and the Africa quote is from "Payback: Bill Martin's Business Acumen Spurs Michigan Athletics to New Heights," *Dividend* (Spring 2005).

20. The Warde Manual quote about why he entered the MBA program is from "From the Locker Room to the Boardroom," *Dividend* (Fall, 2016).

21. The *Wall Street Journal* article mentioning Michigan's well-rounded students is "The Real World" (September 22, 2004).

Chapter 12. The Secret Sauce at Michigan Ross

In addition to the general sources listed previously, sources include the following:

Notes

1. The quotations from alumni GS Suri and Kendall Verbeek are from Michigan Ross alumni profiles: https://michiganross.umich.edu/alumni/alumni-news/alumni-profiles.

2. Information on the early days of alumni activity is from the Ross Records, 1916–2017, at the Bentley Historical Library.

3. For additional information on the founding of the William Davidson Institute, see the WDI publication *A Force for Economic and Social Freedom*: https://wdi.umich.edu/25th-book/?page=1. This publication is the source of the Wilhelme quote.

4. The CK Prahalad quote at the chapter's conclusion is from "Marketing: Selling to the Poor," *Time* (April 17, 2005).

Figure Credits

1. The About the Author photo and Figures I.1, 1.2, 4.1, 10.1, and 12.1 are from my collection. Thank you to Becca Portney for providing the picture of Prince Charles.

2. The following figures are from the Bentley Historical Library:

    Figure 1.1: https://quod.lib.umich.edu/cgi/i/image/image-idx?id=S-BHL-X-HS6199%5DHS6199

    Figure 2.2: https://quod.lib.umich.edu/cgi/i/image/image-idx?id=S-BHL-X-HS460%5DHS460

    Figure 3.1 (also used on the cover): https://quod.lib.umich.edu/cgi/i/image/image-idx?id=S-BHL-X-HS19318%5DHS19318

    Figure 5.1: https://quod.lib.umich.edu/cgi/i/image/image-idx?id=S-BHL-X-HS3716%5DHS3716

    Figure 6.1: https://quod.lib.umich.edu/cgi/i/image/image-idx?id=S-BHL-X-BL005617%5DBL005617

    Figure 7.1: https://quod.lib.umich.edu/cgi/i/image/image-idx?id=S-BHL-X-HS6201%5DHS6201

    Figure 8.1: https://quod.lib.umich.edu/cgi/i/image/image-idx?id=S-BHL-X-HS6203%5DHS6203

Figure Credits

Figure 11.1: https://quod.lib.umich.edu/cgi/i/image/image-idx?id=S-BHL-X-BL000107%5DBL000107

Figure 11.2: https://quod.lib.umich.edu/cgi/i/image/image-idx?id=S-BHL-X-BL003181%5DBL003181

3. Figure 2.1 is from the Ross Business School Records, Box 95, at the Bentley Historical Library.

4. Figure 4.2 was provided by the Ross School of Business.

5. Figure 7.2 is from the U-M News and Information Services photograph series D (faculty and staff portraits), Box 2, at the Bentley Historical Library.

6. Figure 9.1 was provided by Deepa Prahalad.

7. The book's Ross School of Business building cover image was provided by the Ross School of Business.